Manifesto of the Communist Party

A Modern Edition

Karl Marx and Friedrich Engels

With an Introduction by Tariq Ali

VERSO

London • New York

This paperback edition first published 2022
First published by Verso 2016
Introductions © Tariq Ali 2016, 2022
Notes to the *Manifesto* © Eric Hobsbawm 1998, 2016, 2022
'The April Theses' translation © Bernard Isaacs 1964, 2016, 2022
'Letters from Afar' translation © M. S. Levin, Joe Fineberg et al.
Manifesto of the Communist Party first published in English 1848;
this translation first published 1888
'The April Theses [The Tasks of the Proletariat in the Present
Revolution]' first published in *Pravda* no. 26, 7 April 1917; published in
English in V. I. Lenin, *Collected Works*, Vol. 24, 4th ed. (Moscow 1964)
'Letters from Afar' published in English in Lenin, *Collected Works*, Vol. 23

1 3 5 7 9 10 8 6 4 2

Verso
UK: 6 Meard Street, London W1F 0EG
US: 20 Jay Street, Suite 1010, Brooklyn, NY 11201
versobooks.com

Verso is the imprint of New Left Books

ISBN-13: 978-1-83976-423-3
ISBN-13: 978-1-78478-689-2 (UK EBK)
ISBN-13: 978-1-78478-691-5 (US EBK)

British Library Cataloguing in Publication Data
A catalogue record for this book is available from the British Library

Library of Congress Cataloging-in-Publication Data
A catalog record for this book is available from the Library of Congress

Typeset in Bembo by MJ & N Gavan, Truro, Cornwall
Printed and bound by CPI Group (UK) Ltd, Croydon CR0 4YY

Introduction to the Communist Manifesto

Tariq Ali

In Brecht's famous parable of the Tailor of Ulm ... this sixteenth-century German artisan had been obsessed by the idea of building a device that would allow men to fly. One day, convinced that he had succeeded, he took his contraption to the Bishop and said, 'Look, I can fly.' Challenged to prove it, the tailor launched himself into the air from the top of the church roof, and naturally, ended up in smithereens on the paving stones below. And yet, Brecht's poem suggests: a few centuries later men did indeed learn to fly.

Lucio Magri, 'The Tailor of Ulm'

The *Manifesto* is the last great document of the European Enlightenment and the first to register a completely new system of thought: historical materialism. As such it marks both a continuation and a break. Infinitely more radical than its French and American predecessors, written at a time when the impact of a huge political defeat was beginning to wear off, it was the product of two young German minds, both intellectuals in their twenties and both schooled in the Hegelian philosophical tradition that dominated Berlin and other German universities during the first half of the nineteenth century. This text was a major turning point in the revolutionary theory and practice of the last two centuries, insisting, as it does, that revolution is the inevitable outcome of capitalism in modern industrialized societies.

Occasionally, philosophical debates in Germany left a mark much uglier than the duelling scars of the era. It was the evolution of philosophy that resulted in the birth of a new left radical milieu in which Marx and Engels played a significant role. All their texts, especially this one, should be studied in the social, economic and philosophical context of the period in which they were written. To treat them as devotional tracts is to debase both meaning and method and, in the case of the *Manifesto* in particular, to render them harmless. The prescriptions and predictions are obviously outdated today, and capitalism itself, despite the triumph of 1991, appears more like a nervous disorder rather than an organism capable of taking humanity forward. We desperately need a new manifesto to meet the challenges of today and those that lie ahead, but till that time (and even afterwards) there is much to learn from the method, the élan and the language of this one.

Politics was decisive in pushing forward the further radicalization of the young German intelligentsia of the nineteenth century. There was no option left. Either they joined him or they had to move beyond Hegel. The period opened up by the French Revolution in 1789 had come to an end with Napoleon's defeat at

Waterloo in 1815. The Congress of Victors convened in Vienna later that year had agreed a map of Europe and discussed mechanisms through which dissent could be controlled and crushed. The Vienna Consensus would be policed by Russia, Prussia and Austria with the British Navy as an ever-reliable backdrop, a weapon of last resort.[1] The triumph of reaction fuelled the retreat on the intellectual front. Hegel, the theorist of permanent mobility, insisted that history was never static, itself the result of a clash of ideas, a dialectic where past and present determined the future. This history, he insisted, was inevitable,

---

1 Worth recalling that the powerful English fleet itself was the creation of the Commonwealth and the English revolution. Trade routes needed protection and the merchants of the City were happy to fund a strong maritime force that could challenge both pirates and the Dutch. Reminiscing on its history during the Second World War, Churchill acknowledged the debt owed to Cromwell and recalled that, as First Lord of the Admiralty, he had wanted to name a battleship *Cromwell*, but was overruled by George V. In WW2 he was of course in a stronger position, but the C-class destroyer was not completed before the end of the war, and sold the next year to Norway.

unpredictable and, most importantly, unstoppable. Shaken by the defeat at Waterloo, he now accepted the 'end of history'. The once dynamic 'world-spirit' had cast aside Napoleon's greatcoat, hat and the tricolour in favour of the steel helmets and the eagle of the Prussian *Junkers*. Field Marshal Blücher had defeated the upstart Corsican. A triumphant Prussia could well be a model state, confining the historical process to an eternal mausoleum. It was not to be.

Apart from all else, even though 1815 imposed a silence on the French Revolution, its social and juridical achievements were essentially maintained: the feudal estates were not restored to their former lords.[2] The liberating impact

---

2 There was no nineteenth-century equivalent of the *Treuhandanstalt*, set up after the fall of the Berlin Wall in 1990 to privatize state property in the former German Democratic Republic and return estates to *Junker* families. National properties in France after 1815 had not been returned to their former owners, and though some were unfairly distributed to the nouveau riche, many revolutionary advances were safeguarded. The contrast with Eastern Europe today could not be more striking.

of the Revolution lived on in the memories of the common people and not just in France. Rousseau's maxim was not forgotten: 'You are lost if you forget that land belongs to no one and its fruits belong to everyone.'

Some of Hegel's most gifted pupils and followers, including our two authors, followed events in France in minute detail. They were aware of the 'Conspiracy of Equals' that had followed the Revolution. The attempt to establish a 'plebeian Vendee' had been defeated and its commonist/communist planners executed. François Babeuf (who had adopted the pseudonym Gracchus) had stabbed himself to escape execution on 26 March 1797. These vibrant histories as well as those of the Revolution itself were eagerly devoured by young radicals in Germany and elsewhere. Secret societies, underground work, resistance, acts of individual violence were commonplace. Debates on what happened to the 'second revolution' in France after Robespierre's defeat by the Thermidorian Reaction never ceased. It was, after all, the language of the radicals, repudiated by the Directory and Napoleon, that anticipated the demands that would later envelop the continent: universal suffrage, separation of church and state, some redistribution of wealth.

That is why, despite the break with post-1815 Hegel, the German radicals, finding his conclusions deficient, carried on using important elements of his method to investigate the world. Intellectual fertility did not end with the master's retreat, and its offspring increased both in volume and content. Feuerbach had turned Hegel on his head, refuting the notion that ideas determined being. He insisted on the opposite: it was being that determined consciousness. Another precocious Left-Hegelian enhanced the critique further. Marx articulated social and class differences that existed within society as a whole. Might these, he enquired, have something to do with the difference in status between the King of Prussia, a Moselle peasant and a factory worker? What was it that produced the ensemble of social relations that highlighted the difference between one class and another? It was this that needed to be further investigated and mapped in order to understand how the world functioned. It was not enough to denounce property as theft or to state that humans were a product of their environment. Who could have fantasized that the 'world-spirit', expelled from its homeland by rampant reaction, would, thanks to Marx and Lenin, end up in Petrograd and Moscow and later travel to other continents and mingle with native spirits?

A wave of repression soon engulfed different corners of the European continent. The rulers were panicked by the re-emergence of the tricolour in France, and the secret police reported growing discontent in many other parts of the country. The East was largely occupied, unwillingly, by the Austro-Hungarian and Russian Empires. Here a mood of radical nationalism, a desire for self-determination and independence was gaining popularity. The euphoria created by the Congress of Victors had faded—it had never gripped the masses in any case—and various forms of dissent were beginning to appear in the shape of class struggle, democratic demands, and radical nationalism; the mood of the European elites became sombre (not unlike the gatherings of the wealthy and the powerful in Davos and elsewhere after the Wall Street crash of 2008). Even the slightest resistance was seen as a threat to the new order and already limited political rights were further truncated, culminating in severe curbs on freedoms of press, speech and action. Marx was forced into exile, first France, then Belgium and finally England. Engels's family already owned a firm in Manchester, so his choice of exile was predetermined. Other colleagues abandoned Europe altogether and emigrated to the United States where they remained active and maintained regular contact with their comrades in Europe. Many of them put enormous pressure on Marx to migrate to the United States. He resisted for political reasons, seeing Western Europe—the most advanced segment of capitalism—as the epicentre of the revolutions that lay ahead.

Marx would have preferred to live in France,

a country that had become a pole of intellectual and political attraction when he was still growing up in Trier. He had read the works of the Count de Saint-Simon with a mixture of fascination and excitement, and it was in his writings that socialism as a word and an embryonic concept was first encountered. The socialist tradition in France would become deeply rooted only when the industrialization of the country enabled the links between radical ideas and the emergence of a new social layer. A nervous bourgeoisie was not unaware of this, which is why it had introduced the September laws of 1835 that severely curtailed the function of juries and the press. Those who agitated against private property or the state were subjected to harsh penalties. Bourgeois revolutions were going back on their own watchwords and the new bourgeoisie—the 'ultras' so despised by Stendhal—had to be confronted and defeated. This meant moving beyond the limits of German philosophy—Hegel and Feuerbach were not enough. For if meaningful progress was to be achieved the obvious limitations of the propertied elites in modern Europe (England, France, Belgium and Holland) had to be transcended as well.

In an illuminating essay published four years before the *Manifesto* was written, Marx argued that 'clearly the weapon of criticism cannot replace the criticism of weapons … material force can only be overthrown by material force. But theory also becomes a material force when it has gripped the masses.'[3] For both him and Engels it was the 'positive' transcendence of religion that made human beings truly radical, for only then could they become self-reliant, only then could they understand that they and they alone were the supreme being. The major reference point was, of course, the French Revolution, but these new radicals were very conscious of the German history they lived and breathed. If, during the

---

3 'A Contribution to the Critique of Hegel's Philosophy of Right. Introduction', *Karl Marx: Early Writings*, trans. Rodney Livingstone and Gregor Benton (London 1974), p. 243.

German Reformation, it was the monk who had seized the initiative and challenged Rome, it was the philosopher who would now challenge the new powers. Germany, in order to be fully emancipated, had to go beyond what Britain, Holland and France had already achieved.

The *Manifesto* was commissioned as the founding programme of the Communist League, a *foco* of largely German exiles and a few Belgian and English supporters who met in London in the summer of 1847. The Central Committee instructed Marx, then in Brussels, to produce a manifesto. Marx agreed but did not treat the injunction as a priority. He found it easier to complete texts when there was a strict deadline. A few months later a somewhat tetchy triumvirate—citizens Karl Schapper, Heinrich Bauer and Joseph Moll—did suggest a cut-off date and threatened reprisals if it was not met:

> The Central Committee (in London) hereby directs the District Committee of Brussels to

notify Citizen Marx that if the Manifesto of the Communist Party, which he consented at the last Congress, to draw up, does not reach London before Tuesday, February 1 [1848], further measures will be taken against him. In case Citizen Marx does not write the Manifesto, the Central Committee requests the immediate return of the documents that were turned over to him by the Congress.

They were right to be angry. Information reaching them from several European capitals revealed seething discontent, especially among workers, against the 1815 Vienna Consensus. A democratic upsurge was predicted for Germany. The citizens were desperate for a manifesto that could both express the hopes and channel the political energies of the workers. So what on earth was Marx up to? To be fair he was working on the document, but kept being interrupted by German workers and intellectuals who were eager to discuss the situation at home. Marx was instinctively aware that this document was of some importance. For that reason, each word had to carefully weighed, each sentence revised to perfection. This is exactly what he and Engels were engaged in, and it is this, as many have remarked, that gave the document its compelling literary power.

The final version was finished in the first week of February 1848 and it was still hot off the presses as the 1848 revolution erupted in France and spread rapidly to the rest of the continent. The *Manifesto* had no part in preparing or fomenting the struggles, but it was widely circulated and read by those who had played a leading role or participated in the upheavals that lit Europe that year. In the decades that followed it would become the de facto founding document of most social-democrat parties, with Britain (untouched by 1848) as the most important exception. No such party ever came into existence in the United States, where the *Manifesto* was first published in Chicago's German-language press in 1872.

Both Anglo-imperialisms were on the march in February 1848. The British had defeated the

Sikh armies in the previous month and were consolidating their hold on Northern India. A few decades earlier, they had crushed Tipu Sultan, the enlightened Muslim ruler of Mysore in the South who, signing himself as 'Citizen Tipu', had appealed to Napoleon for help against the British. None was forthcoming though friendly letters were exchanged.[4]

In the United States, a warmongering President Polk was seizing Mexican lands—the Californias and New Mexico—and contemplating taking the whole country.[5] The nation's less privileged

---

4 The British General who defeated Tipu Sultan in 1799 was Arthur Wellesley. In a later reincarnation (as the Duke of Wellington), he would also settle accounts with Napoleon in 1815.

5 He did not do so for contingent reasons, confiding to his diary on 21 February 1848, 'A majority of one branch of the Congress is opposed to my administration. They have falsely charged that the war was brought on and is continued by me with a view to the conquest of Mexico, and if I were now to reject a treaty made upon my own terms as authorised in April last, with the unanimous approbation of the Cabinet, the probability is that Congress would grant neither the men nor the money to

citizens were also engaged in conquests and were, for the time being, immunized against the more radical message of the *Manifesto*. As instruments of expansionist capitalism, however, they were fulfilling its predictions of how this newest mode of production would sweep aside everything that stood in its way: native populations, entire countries, ancient traditions. The question not posed was whether those who worked and died for such a system could also become its gravediggers. It was assumed that they would, but they never did. Despite the difference in historical traditions, no imperialist state—Britain, France, Holland,

---

prosecute the war. Should this be the result, the army now in Mexico would be constantly wasting and diminishing in numbers, and I might at last be compelled to withdraw them, and then lose the two provinces of New Mexico and Upper California which were ceded to the US by this treaty.' It was a semi-Hegelian interpretation of the dialectic of imperial conquests: should we go further knowing full well there is a serious possibility that we might lose what we have already conquered? The gold rush of 1849 vindicated Polk's decision. Had the borders been taken any further the 100,000 would-be gringo gold miners might have found the mines already occupied.

Belgium or the United States—ever came close to a socialist revolution. Germany, a wannabe hegemon, did experience serious upheavals but ultimately capital ensured the triumph of the Right. The combination of capital and mass-based fascism combined to destroy all hopes in Italy and Germany. Historical inevitability turned out to be the weak link of this document.

What can one say about its language that has not been said before? Very little. In a previous introduction to this pamphlet, Eric Hobsbawm described how some of its most attractive features lay in its 'passionate conviction, the concentrated brevity, the intellectual and stylistic force ... in lapidary sentences almost naturally transforming themselves into the memorable aphorisms which have become known far beyond the world of political debate'. He pointed out how uncommon this was in nineteenth-century German literature.[6] The content was, as Lenin suggested, a remarkable synthesis of German philosophy,

6   London and New York 1998.

English economics and French politics that had framed the consciousness of its two authors. The lyrical praise of the transforming capacities of capitalism that had 'accomplished wonders far surpassing Egyptian pyramids, Roman aqueducts and Gothic cathedrals' was to emphasize what capitalism's successor could achieve. The new wonders of the world were proudly asserted to demonstrate the forward march of history:

The bourgeoisie, during its role of scarce one hundred years, has created more massive and more colossal productive forces than have all preceding generations together. Subjection of Nature's forces to man, machinery, application of chemistry to industry and agriculture, steam navigation, railways, electric telegraphs, clearings of whole continents for cultivation, canalizing of rivers, whole populations conjured out of the ground—what earlier century had even a presentiment that such productive forces slumbered in the lap of social labour.

Could a socialist revolution built on these foundations transform the 'realm of necessity' into the 'realm of freedom'? History vindicated very few of the predictions contained in the *Manifesto*. Its strength lay in its broad sweep, a call to transform the world. But divisions within the proletariat—pay grades, reserve armies of the unemployed, religion, nationalism, etc.—in the very heartlands of capital, as Marx later recognized in most cases, was not something that could easily be conjured out of existence. Sociology was insufficient. Politics was essential. Famously, Marx and Engels left no detailed blueprint of what a socialist or communist society should look like, something that led academic Marxists to pronounce that Marx's originality lay in his philosophy and economics. Others utilized his panegyrics celebrating the revolutionary capacities of capital to argue that the gravediggers were the capitalists themselves. Best to watch from the sidelines as they committed collective suicide. More recently, before the 2008 Wall Street crash, not an insignificant number of onetime Marxists celebrated the latest 'globalization' as a vindication of Marx. And so they became its mouthpieces and turned their coats with a clear conscience, regarding 2008 as a temporary blip that would soon be transcended and forgotten. The crash brought Marx to the fore again. Not the co-author of the *Manifesto*, but the Marx of *Capital*, who had meticulously analysed this mode of production in greater detail than anyone before or since.

Questions remained. What of those countries that constituted a large majority of the world and where the proletariat was dwarfed by other social layers and was too insignificant economically, socially and politically? Could it spark off a revolution by itself when the overwhelming forces in society were ranged against it? This issue would be hotly debated within international social-democracy in the period that led to the first large-scale inter-imperialist war of 1914–1918. The participants included Lenin. He understood Marx better than most. He had also grasped something that eluded his European colleagues: in times of severe crisis, the 'weakest link in the capitalist chain' would break first, triggering a more general collapse of the system. In April 1917, between the two revolutions that transformed Tsarist Russia during the first imperialist war, he wrote a set of theses, urging his own party to make the necessary preparations for a social revolution. These are included on the flip side of this book to which you may now turn. For without the Russian Revolution of November 1917, the *Communist Manifesto* would have been confined to specialist libraries instead of rivalling the Bible as the most translated text in modern history.

Paris
May 2016

Manifesto of the Communist Party

Karl Marx and Friedrich Engels

A spectre is haunting Europe—the spectre of Communism. All the powers of old Europe have entered into a holy alliance to exorcize this spectre: Pope and Tsar, Metternich[1] and Guizot,[2] French radicals and German police spies.

Where is the party in opposition that has not

---

1 Clemens Lothar, Prince Metternich, was the leading Austrian statesman from 1809 to 1848 and the architect of the counter-revolutionary Holy Alliance.

2 François Guizot was a French historian and de facto Prime Minister from 1840 to 1848 under the Orleanist 'July' monarchy of Louis Phillipe.

been decried as communistic by its opponents in power? Where the opposition that has not hurled back the branding reproach of Communism, against the more advanced opposition parties, as well as against its reactionary adversaries?

Two things result from this fact:

1. Communism is already acknowledged by all European powers to be itself a power.
2. It is high time that Communists should openly, in the face of the whole world, publish their views, their aims, their tendencies, and meet this nursery tale of the Spectre of Communism with a manifesto of the party itself.

To this end, Communists of various nationalities have assembled in London, and sketched the following manifesto, to be published in the English, French, German, Italian, Flemish and Danish languages.

I. Bourgeois and Proletarians[3]

The history of all hitherto existing society[4] is the history of class struggles.

---

3   By bourgeoisie is meant the class of modern capitalists, owners of the means of social production and employers of wage labour. By proletariat, the class of modern wage labourers who, having no means of production of their own, are reduced to selling their labour power in order to live [Engels].

4   That is, all *written* history. In 1847, the pre-history of society, the social organization existing previous to recorded history, was all but unknown. Since then, Haxthausen discovered common ownership of land in Russia, Maurer proved it to be the social foundation from which all Teutonic races started in history, and by and by village communities were found to be, or to have been, the primitive form of society everywhere from India to Ireland. The inner organization of this primitive communistic society was laid bare, in its typical form, by Morgan's crowning discovery of the true nature of the *gens* and its relation to the *tribe*. With the dissolution of these primeval communities society begins to be differentiated into separate and finally antagonistic classes. I have attempted to retrace this process of dissolution in *Der Ursprung der Familie, des Privateigenthums und des Staats* (The Origin of the Family, Private Property, and the State) [Engels].

Freeman and slave, patrician and plebeian, lord and serf, guild-master[5] and journeyman, in a word, oppressor and oppressed, stood in constant opposition to one another, carried on an uninterrupted, now hidden, now open fight, a fight that each time ended, either in a revolutionary reconstitution of society at large, or in the common ruin of the contending classes.

In the earlier epochs of history, we find almost everywhere a complicated arrangement of society into various orders, a manifold gradation of social rank. In ancient Rome we have patricians, knights, plebeians, slaves; in the Middle Ages, feudal lords, vassals, guild-masters, journeymen, apprentices, serfs; in almost all of these classes, again, subordinate gradations.

The modern bourgeois society that has sprouted from the ruins of feudal society has not done away with class antagonisms. It has but established new classes, new conditions of oppression, new forms of struggle in place of the old ones.

---

5 Guild-master, that is, a full member of a guild, a master within, not a head of a guild [Engels].

Our epoch, the epoch of the bourgeoisie, possesses, however, this distinctive feature: it has simplified the class antagonisms. Society as a whole is more and more splitting up into two great hostile camps, into two great classes directly facing each other: bourgeoisie and proletariat.

From the serfs of the Middle Ages sprang the chartered burghers of the earliest towns. From these burgesses the first elements of the bourgeoisie were developed.

The discovery of America, the rounding of the Cape, opened up fresh ground for the rising bourgeoisie. The East Indian and Chinese markets, the colonization of America, trade with the colonies, the increase in the means of exchange and in commodities generally, gave to commerce, to navigation, to industry, an impulse never before known, and thereby, to the revolutionary element in the tottering feudal society, a rapid development.

The feudal system of industry, under which industrial production was monopolized by closed guilds, now no longer sufficed for the growing wants of the new markets. The manufacturing system took its place. The guild-masters were pushed on one side by the manufacturing middle class; division of labour between the different corporate guilds vanished in the face of division of labour in each single workshop.

Meantime the markets kept ever growing, the demand ever rising. Even manufacture no longer sufficed. Thereupon, steam and machinery revolutionized industrial production. The place of manufacture was taken by the giant, modern industry, the place of the industrial middle class, by industrial millionaires, the leaders of whole industrial armies, the modern bourgeois.

Modern industry has established the world market, for which the discovery of America paved the way. This market has given an immense development to commerce, to navigation, to communication by land. This development has, in its turn, reacted on the extension of industry; and in proportion as industry, commerce, navigation, railways extended, in the same proportion the bourgeoisie developed, increased its capital, and pushed into the background every class handed down from the Middle Ages.

We see, therefore, how the modern bourgeoisie is itself the product of a long course of development, of a series of revolutions in the modes of production and of exchange.

Each step in the development of the bourgeoisie was accompanied by a corresponding political advance of that class. An oppressed class under the sway of the feudal nobility, an armed and self-governing association in the medieval commune;[6] here independent urban republic (as in Italy and Germany), there taxable 'third estate' of the monarchy (as in France), afterwards, in the period of manufacture proper, serving either the semi-feudal or the absolute monarchy as a counterpoise against the nobility, and, in fact,

---

6 'Commune' was the name taken, in France, by the nascent towns even before they had conquered, from their feudal lords and masters, local self-government and political rights as the 'third estate'. Generally speaking, for the economic development of the bourgeoisie, England is here taken as the typical country; for its political development, France [Engels].

cornerstone of the great monarchies in general, the bourgeoisie has at last, since the establishment of modern industry and of the world market, conquered for itself, in the modern representative state, exclusive political sway. The executive of the modern state is but a committee for managing the common affairs of the whole bourgeoisie.

The bourgeoisie, historically, has played a most revolutionary part.

The bourgeoisie, wherever it has got the upper hand, has put an end to all feudal, patriarchal, idyllic relations. It has pitilessly torn asunder the motley feudal ties that bound man to his 'natural superiors', and has left remaining no other nexus between man and man than naked self-interest, than callous 'cash payment'. It has drowned the most heavenly ecstasies of religious fervour, of chivalrous enthusiasm, of philistine sentimentalism, in the icy water of egotistical calculation. It has resolved personal worth into exchange value, and in place of the numberless indefeasible chartered freedoms, has set up that single, unconscionable freedom—free trade. In one word, for exploitation, veiled by religious and political illusions, it has substituted naked, shameless, direct, brutal exploitation.

The bourgeoisie has stripped of its halo every occupation hitherto honoured and looked up to with reverent awe. It has converted the physician, the lawyer, the priest, the poet, the man of science, into its paid wage labourers.

The bourgeoisie has torn away from the family its sentimental veil, and has reduced the family relation to a mere money relation.

The bourgeoisie has disclosed how it came to pass that the brutal display of vigour in the Middle Ages, which reactionists so much admire, found its fitting complement in the most slothful indolence. It has been the first to show what man's activity can bring about. It has accomplished wonders far surpassing Egyptian pyramids, Roman aqueducts, and Gothic cathedrals; it has conducted expeditions that put in the shade all former exoduses of nations and crusades.

The bourgeoisie cannot exist without constantly revolutionizing the instruments of production, and thereby the relations of production, and with them the whole relations of society. Conservation of the old modes of production in unaltered form, was, on the contrary, the first condition of existence for all earlier industrial classes. Constant revolutionizing of production, uninterrupted disturbance of all social conditions, everlasting uncertainty and agitation distinguish the bourgeois epoch from all earlier ones. All fixed, fast-frozen relations, with their train of ancient and venerable prejudices and opinions, are swept away, all new-formed ones become antiquated before they can ossify. All that is solid melts into air, all that is holy is profaned, and man is at last compelled to face with sober senses, his real conditions of life, and his relations with his kind.

The need of a constantly expanding market for its products chases the bourgeoisie over the whole surface of the globe. It must nestle everywhere, settle everywhere, establish connections everywhere.

The bourgeoisie has through its exploitation of the world market given a cosmopolitan character to production and consumption in every country. To the great chagrin of reactionists, it has drawn from under the feet of industry the national ground on which it stood. All old-established national industries have been destroyed or are daily being destroyed. They are dislodged by new industries, whose introduction becomes a life and death question for all civilized nations, by industries that no longer work up indigenous raw material, but raw material drawn from the remotest zones; industries whose products are consumed, not only at home, but in every quarter of the globe. In place of the old wants, satisfied by the productions of the country, we find new wants, requiring for their satisfaction the products of distant lands and climes. In place of the old local and national seclusion and self-sufficiency, we have intercourse in every direction, universal interdependence of nations. And as in material, so also in intellectual production. The intellectual creations of individual nations become common property. National one-sidedness and narrow-mindedness become more and more impossible, and from the numerous national and local literatures, there arises a world literature.

The bourgeoisie, by the rapid improvement of all instruments of production, by the immensely facilitated means of communication, draws all, even the most barbarian, nations into civilization. The cheap prices of its commodities are the heavy artillery with which it batters down all Chinese walls, with which it forces the barbarians' intensely obstinate hatred of foreigners to capitulate. It compels all nations, on pain of extinction, to adopt the bourgeois mode of production; it compels them to introduce what it calls civilization into their midst, i.e., to become bourgeois themselves. In one word, it creates a world after its own image.

The bourgeoisie has subjected the country to the rule of the towns. It has created enormous cities, has greatly increased the urban population as compared with the rural, and has thus rescued a considerable part of the population from the idiocy of rural life. Just as it has made the country dependent on the towns, so it has made barbarian and semi-barbarian countries dependent on the civilized ones, nations of peasants on nations of bourgeois, the East on the West.

The bourgeoisie keeps more and more doing away with the scattered state of the population, of the means of production, and of property. It has agglomerated population, centralized means of production, and has concentrated property in a few hands. The necessary consequence of this was political centralization. Independent, or but loosely connected provinces, with separate interests, laws, governments and systems of taxation, became lumped together into one nation, with one government, one code of laws, one national class interest, one frontier and one customs tariff.

The bourgeoisie, during its rule of scarce one hundred years, has created more massive and more colossal productive forces than have all preceding generations together. Subjection of nature's forces to man, machinery, application of chemistry to industry and agriculture, steam navigation, railways, electric telegraphs, clearing of whole continents for cultivation, canalization of rivers, whole populations conjured out of the ground—what earlier century had even a pre-sentiment that such productive forces slumbered in the lap of social labour?

We see then: the means of production and of exchange, on whose foundation the bourgeoisie built itself up, were generated in feudal society. At a certain stage in the development of these means of production and of exchange, the con-ditions under which feudal society produced and exchanged, the feudal organization of agriculture and manufacturing industry, in one word, the feudal relations of property became no longer compatible with the already developed produc-tive forces; they became so many fetters. They had to be burst asunder; they were burst asunder.

Into their place stepped free competition, accompanied by a social and political constitu-tion adapted to it, and by the economical and political sway of the bourgeois class.

A similar movement is going on before our own eyes. Modern bourgeois society with its relations of production, of exchange and of property, a society that has conjured up such gigantic means of production and of exchange, is like the sorcerer, who is no longer able to control the powers of the nether world whom he has called up by his spells. For many a decade past, the history of industry and commerce is but the history of the revolt of modern productive forces against modern conditions of production, against the property relations that are the conditions for the existence of the bourgeoisie and of its rule. It is enough to mention the commercial crises that by their periodical return put on trial, each time more threateningly, the existence of the entire bourgeois society. In these crises a great part not only of the existing products, but also of the previously created productive forces, are periodically destroyed. In these crises there breaks out an epidemic that, in all earlier epochs, would have seemed an absurdity—the epidemic of overproduction. Society suddenly finds itself put back into a state of momentary barbarism; it appears as if a famine, a universal war of devastation had cut off the supply of every means of subsistence; industry and commerce seem to be destroyed; and why? Because there is too much civilization, too much means of subsistence, too much industry, too much commerce. The productive forces at the disposal of society no longer tend to further the development of the conditions of bourgeois property; on the contrary, they have become too powerful for these conditions, by which they are fettered, and so soon as they overcome these fetters, they bring disorder into the whole of bourgeois society, endanger the existence of bourgeois property. The conditions of bourgeois society are too narrow to comprise the wealth created by them. And how does the bourgeoisie get over these crises? On the one hand by enforced destruction of a mass of productive forces; on the other, by the conquest of new markets, and by the more thorough exploitation of the old ones. That is to say, by paving the way for more extensive and more destructive crises, and by diminishing the means whereby crises are prevented.

The weapons with which the bourgeoisie felled feudalism to the ground are now turned against the bourgeoisie itself.

But not only has the bourgeoisie forged the weapons that bring death to itself; it has also called into existence the men who are to wield those weapons—the modern working class—the proletarians.

In proportion as the bourgeoisie, i.e., capital, is developed, in the same proportion is the proletariat, the modern working class, developed—a class of labourers, who live only so long as they find work, and who find work only so long as their labour increases capital. These labourers, who must sell themselves piecemeal, are a commodity, like every other article of commerce, and are consequently exposed to all the vicissitudes of competition, to all the fluctuations of the market.

Owing to the extensive use of machinery and to division of labour, the work of the proletarians has lost all individual character, and, consequently, all charm for the workman. He becomes an appendage of the machine, and it is only the most simple, most monotonous, and most easily acquired knack, that is required of him. Hence, the cost of production of a workman is restricted, almost entirely, to the means of subsistence that he requires for his maintenance, and for the propagation of his race. But the price of a commodity, and therefore also of labour,[7] is equal to its cost of production. In proportion, therefore, as the repulsiveness of the work increases, the wage decreases. Nay more, in proportion as the use of machinery and division of labour increases, in the same proportion the burden of toil also increases, whether by prolongation of the working hours, by increase of the work exacted in a given time or by increased speed of the machinery, etc.

Modern industry has converted the little workshop of the patriarchal master into the great factory of the industrial capitalist. Masses of

---

7   In Marx's later theory of surplus value, he concluded that it is the worker's *labour power*, not his labour, that is sold to the capitalist as a commodity. See 'Wages, Prices and Profit' in Marx-Engels, *Selected Works*, Lawrence & Wishart (London 1968).

labourers, crowded into the factory, are organized like soldiers. As privates of the industrial army they are placed under the command of a perfect hierarchy of officers and sergeants. Not only are they slaves of the bourgeois class, and of the bourgeois state; they are daily and hourly enslaved by the machine, by the overseer, and, above all, by the individual bourgeois manufacturer himself. The more openly this despotism proclaims gain to be its end and aim, the more petty, the more hateful and the more embittering it is.

The less the skill and exertion of strength implied in manual labour, in other words, the more modern industry becomes developed, the more is the labour of men superseded by that of women. Differences of age and sex have no longer any distinctive social validity for the working class. All are instruments of labour, more or less expensive to use, according to their age and sex.

No sooner is the exploitation of the labourer by the manufacturer so far at an end that he receives his wages in cash, than he is set upon by the other portions of the bourgeoisie, the landlord, the shopkeeper, the pawnbroker, etc.

The lower strata of the middle class—the small tradespeople, shopkeepers, and *rentiers*, the handicraftsmen and peasants—all these sink gradually into the proletariat, partly because their diminutive capital does not suffice for the scale on which modern industry is carried on, and is swamped in the competition with the large capitalists, partly because their specialized skill is rendered worthless by new methods of production. Thus the proletariat is recruited from all classes of the population.

The proletariat goes through various stages of development. With its birth begins its struggle with the bourgeoisie. At first the contest is carried on by individual labourers, then by the workpeople of a factory, then by the operatives of one trade, in one locality, against the individual bourgeois who directly exploits them. They direct their attacks not against the bourgeois conditions of production, but against the instruments of production themselves; they destroy imported wares that compete with their labour, they smash to pieces machinery, they set factories ablaze, they seek to restore by force the vanished status of the workman of the Middle Ages.

At this stage the labourers still form an incoherent mass scattered over the whole country, and broken up by their mutual competition. If anywhere they unite to form more compact bodies, this is not yet the consequence of their own active union, but of the union of the bourgeoisie, which class, in order to attain its own political ends, is compelled to set the whole proletariat in motion, and is moreover yet, for a time, able to do so. At this stage, therefore, the proletarians do not fight their enemies, but the enemies of their enemies, the remnants of absolute monarchy, the landowners, the non-industrial bourgeois, the petty bourgeoisie. Thus the whole historical movement is concentrated in the hands of the bourgeoisie; every victory so obtained is a victory for the bourgeoisie.

But with the development of industry the proletariat not only increases in number; it becomes concentrated in greater masses, its strength grows, and it feels that strength more. The various interests and conditions of life within the ranks of the proletariat are more and more equalized, in proportion as machinery obliterates all distinctions of labour, and nearly everywhere reduces wages to the same low level. The growing competition among the bourgeois, and the resulting commercial crises, make the wages of the workers ever more fluctuating. The unceasing improvement of machinery, ever more rapidly developing, makes their livelihood more and more precarious; the collisions between individual workmen and individual bourgeois take more and more the character of collisions between two classes. Thereupon the workers begin to form combinations (trade unions) against the bourgeois; they club together in order to keep up the rate of wages; they found permanent associations in order to make provision beforehand for these occasional revolts. Here and there the contest breaks out into riots.

Now and then the workers are victorious, but only for a time. The real fruit of their battles lies, not in the immediate result, but in the ever expanding union of the workers. This union is helped on by the improved means of communication that are created by modern industry, and that place the workers of different localities in contact with one another. It was just this contact that was needed to centralize the numerous local struggles, all of the same character, into one national struggle between classes. But every class struggle is a political struggle. And that union, to attain which the burghers of the Middle Ages, with their miserable highways, required centuries, the modern proletarians, thanks to railways, achieve in a few years.

This organization of the proletarians into a class, and consequently into a political party, is continually being upset again by the competition between the workers themselves. But it ever rises up again, stronger, firmer, mightier. It compels legislative recognition of particular interests of the workers, by taking advantage of the divisions among the bourgeoisie itself. Thus the Ten Hours Bill in England was carried.[8]

---

8   In 1846. See Engels's article 'The English Ten Hours

Altogether, collisions between the classes of the old society further, in many ways, the course of development of the proletariat. The bourgeoisie finds itself involved in a constant battle: at first with the aristocracy; later on, with those portions of the bourgeoisie itself, whose interests have become antagonistic to the progress of industry; at all times, with the bourgeoisie of foreign countries. In all these battles it sees itself compelled to appeal to the proletariat, to ask for its help, and thus to drag it into the political arena. The bourgeoisie itself, therefore, supplies the proletariat with its own elements of political and general education, in other words, it furnishes the proletariat with weapons for fighting the bourgeoisie.

Further, as we have already seen, entire sections of the ruling classes are, by the advance of industry, precipitated into the proletariat, or are at least threatened in their conditions of existence. These also supply the proletariat with fresh elements of enlightenment and progress.

Bill', Marx-Engels, *Articles on Britain*, Progress Publishers (Moscow 1971), pp. 96–108.

Finally, in times when the class struggle nears the decisive hour, the process of dissolution going on within the ruling class, in fact within the whole range of old society, assumes such a violent, glaring character, that a small section of the ruling class cuts itself adrift, and joins the revolutionary class, the class that holds the future in its hands. Just as, therefore, at an earlier period, a section of the nobility went over to the bourgeoisie, so now a portion of the bourgeoisie goes over to the proletariat, and in particular, a portion of the bourgeois ideologists, who have raised themselves to the level of comprehending theoretically the historical movement as a whole.

Of all the classes that stand face to face with the bourgeoisie today, the proletariat alone is a really revolutionary class. The other classes decay and finally disappear in the face of modern industry; the proletariat is its special and essential product.

The lower middle class, the small manufacturer, the shopkeeper, the artisan, the peasant, all these fight against the bourgeoisie, to save from extinction their existence as fractions of the

middle class. They are therefore not revolutionary, but conservative. Nay more, they are reactionary, for they try to roll back the wheel of
history. If by chance they are revolutionary, they
are so only in view of their impending transfer
into the proletariat, they thus defend not their
present, but their future interests, they desert
their own standpoint to place themselves at that
of the proletariat.

The 'dangerous class',[9] the social scum, that
passively rotting mass thrown off by the lowest
layers of old society, may, here and there, be swept
into the movement by a proletarian revolution;
its conditions of life, however, prepare it far
more for the part of a bribed tool of reactionary
intrigue.

In the conditions of the proletariat, those of
old society at large are already virtually swamped.
The proletarian is without property; his relation
to his wife and children has no longer anything

---

9 That is, the lumpenproletariat of casual labourers
and unemployed, which was very extensive in the cities of
nineteenth-century Europe.

in common with the bourgeois family relations; modern industrial labour, modern subjection to capital, the same in England as in France, in America as in Germany, has stripped him of every trace of national character. Law, morality, religion, are to him so many bourgeois prejudices, behind which lurk in ambush just as many bourgeois interests.

All the preceding classes that got the upper hand, sought to fortify their already acquired status by subjecting society at large to their conditions of appropriation. The proletarians cannot become masters of the productive forces of society, except by abolishing their own previous mode of appropriation, and thereby also every other previous mode of appropriation. They have nothing of their own to secure and to fortify; their mission is to destroy all previous securities for, and insurances of, individual property.

All previous historical movements were movements of minorities, or in the interest of minorities. The proletarian movement is the self-conscious, independent movement of the immense majority, in the interest of the immense majority. The proletariat, the lowest stratum of our present society, cannot stir, cannot raise itself up, without the whole superincumbent strata of official society being sprung into the air.

Though not in substance, yet in form, the struggle of the proletariat with the bourgeoisie is at first a national struggle. The proletariat of each country must, of course, first of all settle matters with its own bourgeoisie.

In depicting the most general phases of the development of the proletariat, we traced the more or less veiled civil war, raging within existing society, up to the point where that war breaks out into open revolution, and where the violent overthrow of the bourgeoisie lays the foundation for the sway of the proletariat.

Hitherto, every form of society has been based, as we have already seen, on the antagonism of oppressing and oppressed classes. But in order to oppress a class, certain conditions must be assured to it under which it can, at least, continue its slavish existence. The serf, in the period of serfdom, raised himself to membership in the commune, just as the petty bourgeois, under the yoke of feudal absolutism, managed to develop into a bourgeois. The modern labourer, on the contrary, instead of rising with the progress of industry, sinks deeper and deeper below the conditions of existence of his own class. He becomes a pauper, and pauperism develops more rapidly than population and wealth. And here it becomes evident that the bourgeoisie is unfit any longer to be the ruling class in society, and to impose its conditions of existence upon society as an overriding law. It is unfit to rule because it is incompetent to assure an existence to its slave within his slavery, because it cannot help letting him sink into such a state that it has to feed him, instead of being fed by him. Society can no longer live under this bourgeoisie, in other words, its existence is no longer compatible with society.

The essential condition for the existence, and for the sway of the bourgeois class, is the formation and augmentation of capital; the condition for capital is wage labour. Wage labour rests exclusively on competition between the labourers. The advance of industry, whose involuntary promoter is the bourgeoisie, replaces the isolation of the labourers, due to competition, by their revolutionary combination, due to association. The development of modern industry, therefore, cuts from under its feet the very foundation on which the bourgeoisie produces and appropriates products. What the bourgeoisie therefore produces, above all, are its own grave-diggers. Its fall and the victory of the proletariat are equally inevitable.

II. Proletarians and Communists

In what relation do the Communists stand to the proletarians as a whole?

The Communists do not form a separate party opposed to other working-class parties.

They have no interests separate and apart from those of the proletariat as a whole.

The Communists are distinguished from the other working-class parties by this only:

1. In the national struggles of the proletarians of the different countries, they point out and bring to the front the common interests of the entire proletariat, independently of all nationality.
2. In the various stages of development which the struggle of the working class against the bourgeoisie has to pass through, they always and everywhere represent the interests of the movement as a whole.

The Communists, therefore, are on the one hand, practically, the most advanced and resolute section of the working-class parties of every country, that section which pushes forward all others; on the other hand, theoretically, they have over the great mass of the proletariat the advantage of clearly understanding the line of march, the conditions, and the ultimate general results of the proletarian movement.

The immediate aim of the Communists is the same as that of all the other proletarian parties: formation of the proletariat into a class, overthrow of the bourgeois supremacy, conquest of political power by the proletariat.

The theoretical conclusions of the Communists are in no way based on ideas or principles that have been invented, or discovered, by this or that would-be universal reformer.

They merely express, in general terms, actual relations springing from an existing class struggle, from a historical movement going on under our very eyes. The abolition of existing property relations is not at all a distinctive feature of communism.

All property relations in the past have continually been subject to historical change consequent upon the change in historical conditions.

The French Revolution, for example, abolished feudal property in favour of bourgeois property.

The distinguishing feature of communism is not the abolition of property generally, but the abolition of bourgeois property. But modern bourgeois private property is the final and most complete expression of the system of producing and appropriating products that is based on class antagonisms, on the exploitation of the many by the few.

In this sense, the theory of the Communists may be summed up in the single sentence: Abolition of private property.

We Communists have been reproached with the desire of abolishing the right of personally acquiring property as the fruit of a man's own labour, which property is alleged to be the groundwork of all personal freedom, activity and independence.

Hard-won, self-acquired, self-earned property! Do you mean the property of the petty artisan and of the small peasant, a form of property that preceded the bourgeois form? There is no need to abolish that; the development of industry has to a great extent already destroyed it, and is still destroying it daily.

Or do you mean modern bourgeois private property?

But does wage labour create any property for the labourer? Not a bit. It creates capital, i.e., that kind of property which exploits wage labour, and which cannot increase except upon conditions of begetting a new supply of wage labour for fresh exploitation. Property, in its present form, is based on the antagonism of capital and wage labour. Let us examine both sides of this antagonism.

To be a capitalist is to have not only a purely personal, but a social status in production. Capital is a collective product, and only by the united action of many members, nay, in the last resort, only by the united action of all members of society, can it be set in motion.

Capital is, therefore, not a personal, it is a social power.

When, therefore, capital is converted into common property, into the property of all members of society, personal property is not thereby transformed into social property. It is only the social character of the property that is changed. It loses its class character.

Let us now take wage labour.

The average price of wage labour is the minimum wage, i.e., that quantum of the means of subsistence which is absolutely requisite to keep the labourer in bare existence as a labourer. What, therefore, the wage labourer appropriates by means of his labour, merely suffices to prolong and reproduce a bare existence. We by no means intend to abolish this personal appropriation of the products of labour, an appropriation that is made for the maintenance and reproduction of human life, and that leaves no surplus wherewith to command the labour of others. All that we want to do away with, is the miserable character of this appropriation, under which the labourer lives merely to increase capital, and is allowed to live only in so far as the interest of the ruling class requires it.

In bourgeois society, living labour is but a means to increase accumulated labour. In Communist society, accumulated labour is but a means to widen, to enrich, to promote the existence of the labourer.

In bourgeois society, therefore, the past dominates the present; in Communist society, the present dominates the past. In bourgeois society capital is independent and has individuality, while the living person is dependent and has no individuality.

And the abolition of this state of things is called by the bourgeois, abolition of individuality and freedom! And rightly so. The abolition of bourgeois individuality, bourgeois independence, and bourgeois freedom is undoubtedly aimed at.

By freedom is meant, under the present bourgeois conditions of production, free trade, free selling and buying.

But if selling and buying disappears, free selling and buying disappears also. This talk about free selling and buying, and all the other 'brave words' of our bourgeoisie about freedom in general, have a meaning, if any, only in contrast with restricted selling and buying, with the fettered traders of the Middle Ages, but have no meaning when opposed to the communistic abolition of buying and selling, of the bourgeois conditions of production, and the bourgeoisie itself.

You are horrified at our intending to do away with private property. But in your existing society, private property is already done away with for nine-tenths of the population; its existence for the few is solely due to its non-existence in the hands of those nine-tenths. You reproach us, therefore, with intending to do away with a form of property, the necessary condition for whose existence is the non-existence of any property for the immense majority of society.

In one word, you reproach us with intending to do away with your property. Precisely so; that is just what we intend.

From the moment when labour can no longer be converted into capital, money, or rent, into a social power capable of being monopolized, i.e., from the moment when individual property can no longer be transformed into bourgeois property, into capital, from that moment, you say, individuality vanishes.

You must, therefore, confess that by 'individual' you mean no other person than the bourgeois, than the middle-class owner of property. This person must, indeed, be swept out of the way, and made impossible.

Communism deprives no man of the power to appropriate the products of society; all that it does is to deprive him of the power to subjugate the labour of others by means of such appropriation.

It has been objected that upon the abolition of private property all work will cease, and universal laziness will overtake us.

According to this, bourgeois society ought long ago to have gone to the dogs through sheer idleness; for those of its members who work, acquire nothing, and those who acquire anything, do not work. The whole of this objection is but another expression of the tautology that there can no longer be any wage labour when there is no longer any capital.

All objections urged against the communistic mode of producing and appropriating material products have, in the same way, been urged against the communistic mode of producing and appropriating intellectual products. Just as, to the bourgeois, the disappearance of class property is the disappearance of production itself, so the disappearance of class culture is to him identical with the disappearance of all culture.

That culture, the loss of which he laments, is, for the enormous majority, a mere training to act as a machine.

But don't wrangle with us so long as you apply, to our intended abolition of bourgeois property, the standard of your bourgeois notions of freedom, culture, law, etc. Your very ideas are but the outgrowth of the conditions of your bourgeois production and bourgeois property, just as your jurisprudence is but the will of your class made into a law for all, a will whose essential character and direction are determined by the economical conditions of existence of your class.

The selfish misconception that induces you to transform into eternal laws of nature and of reason the social forms springing from your present mode of production and form of property —historical relations that rise and disappear in the progress of production—this misconception you share with every ruling class that has preceded you. What you see clearly in the case of ancient property, what you admit in the case of feudal property, you are of course forbidden to admit in the case of your own bourgeois form of property.

Abolition of the family! Even the most radical flare up at this infamous proposal of the Communists.

On what foundation is the present family, the bourgeois family, based? On capital, on private gain. In its completely developed form this family exists only among the bourgeoisie. But this state of things finds its complement in the practical absence of the family among the proletarians, and in public prostitution.

The bourgeois family will vanish as a matter of course when its complement vanishes, and both will vanish with the vanishing of capital.

Do you charge us with wanting to stop the exploitation of children by their parents? To this crime we plead guilty.

But, you will say, we destroy the most hallowed of relations, when we replace home education by social.

And your education! Is not that also social, and determined by the social conditions under which you educate, by the intervention direct or indirect, of society, by means of schools, etc.? The Communists have not invented the intervention of society in education; they do but seek to alter the character of that intervention, and to rescue education from the influence of the ruling class.

The bourgeois claptrap about the family and education, about the hallowed co-relation of parent and child, becomes all the more disgusting, the more, by the action of modern industry, all family ties among the proletarians are torn asunder, and their children transformed into simple articles of commerce and instruments of labour.

But you Communists would introduce community of women, screams the whole bourgeoisie in chorus.

The bourgeois sees in his wife a mere instrument of production. He hears that the instruments of production are to be exploited in common, and, naturally, can come to no other conclusion than that the lot of being common to all will likewise fall to the women.

He has not even a suspicion that the real point aimed at is to do away with the status of women as mere instruments of production.

For the rest, nothing is more ridiculous than the virtuous indignation of our bourgeois at the community of women which, they pretend, is to be openly and officially established by the Communists. The Communists have no need to introduce community of women; it has existed almost from time immemorial.

Our bourgeois, not content with having the wives and daughters of their proletarians at their disposal, not to speak of common prostitutes, take the greatest pleasure in seducing each other's wives.

Bourgeois marriage is in reality a system of wives in common, and thus, at the most, what the Communists might possibly be reproached with, is that they desire to introduce, in substitution for a hypocritically concealed, an openly legalized community of women. For the rest, it is self-evident that the abolition of the present system of production must bring with it the abolition of the community of women springing from that system, i.e., of prostitution both public and private.

The Communists are further reproached with desiring to abolish countries and nationality.

The working men have no country. We cannot take from them what they have not got. Since the proletariat must first of all acquire political supremacy, must rise to be the leading class of the nation, must constitute itself as the nation, it is, so far, itself national, though not in the bourgeois sense of the word.

National differences, and antagonisms between peoples, are daily more and more vanishing, owing to the development of the bourgeoisie, to freedom of commerce, to the world market, to uniformity in the mode of production and in the conditions of life corresponding thereto.

The supremacy of the proletariat will cause them to vanish still faster. United action, of the leading civilized countries at least, is one of the first conditions for the emancipation of the proletariat.

In proportion as the exploitation of one individual by another is put an end to, the exploitation of one nation by another will also be put an end to. In proportion as the antagonism between classes within the nation vanishes, the hostility of one nation to another will come to an end.

The charges against Communism made from a religious, a philosophical, and, generally, from an ideological standpoint, are not deserving of serious examination.

Does it require deep intuition to comprehend that man's ideas, views and conceptions, in one word, man's consciousness, changes with every change in the conditions of his material existence, in his social relations and in his social life?

What else does the history of ideas prove, than that intellectual production changes its character in proportion as material production is changed? The ruling ideas of each age have ever been the ideas of its ruling class.

When people speak of ideas that revolutionize

society, they do but express the fact that within the old society, the elements of a new one have been created, and that the dissolution of the old ideas keeps even pace with the dissolution of the old conditions of existence.

When the ancient world was in its last throes, the ancient religions were overcome by Christianity. When Christian ideas succumbed in the eighteenth century to rationalist ideas, feudal society fought its death battle with the then revolutionary bourgeoisie. The ideas of religious liberty and freedom of conscience merely gave expression to the sway of free competition within the domain of knowledge.

'Undoubtedly,' it will be said, 'religious, moral, philosophical and juridical ideas have been modified in the course of historical development. But religion, morality, philosophy, political science and law constantly survived this change.

'There are, besides, eternal truths, such as freedom, justice, etc., that are common to all states of society. But Communism abolishes eternal truths, it abolishes all religion and all morality, instead of constituting them on a new basis; it therefore acts in contradiction to all past historical experience.'

What does this accusation reduce itself to? The history of all past society has consisted in the development of class antagonisms, antagonisms that assumed different forms at different epochs.

But whatever form they may have taken, one fact is common to all past ages, viz., the exploitation of one part of society by the other. No wonder, then, that the social consciousness of past ages, despite all the multiplicity and variety it displays, moves within certain common forms, or general ideas, which cannot completely vanish except with the total disappearance of class antagonisms.

The Communist revolution is the most radical rupture with traditional property relations; no wonder that its development involves the most radical rupture with traditional ideas.

But let us have done with the bourgeois objections to Communism. We have seen above, that the first step in the revolution by the working class is to raise the proletariat to the position of ruling class, to win the battle of democracy.

The proletariat will use its political supremacy to wrest, by degrees, all capital from the bourgeoisie, to centralize all instruments of production in the hands of the state, i.e., of the proletariat organized as the ruling class, and to increase the total of productive forces as rapidly as possible.

Of course, in the beginning, this cannot be effected except by means of despotic inroads on the rights of property, and on the conditions of bourgeois production; by means of measures, therefore, which appear economically insufficient and untenable, but which, in the course of the movement, outstrip themselves, necessitate further inroads upon the old social order, and are unavoidable as a means of entirely revolutionizing the mode of production.

These measures will of course be different in different countries.

Nevertheless, in the most advanced countries, the following will be pretty generally applicable:

1. Abolition of property in land and application of all rents of land to public purposes.
2. A heavy progressive or graduated income tax.
3. Abolition of all right of inheritance.
4. Confiscation of the property of all emigrants and rebels.
5. Centralization of credit in the hands of the state, by means of a national bank with state capital and an exclusive monopoly.
6. Centralization of the means of communication and transport in the hands of the state.
7. Extension of factories and instruments of production owned by the state; the bringing into cultivation of waste lands, and the improvement of the soil generally in accordance with a common plan.
8. Equal liability of all to labour. Establishment of industrial armies, especially for agriculture.
9. Combination of agriculture with manufacturing industries; gradual abolition of the distinction between town and country, by a more equable distribution of the population over the country.

10. Free education for all children in public schools. Abolition of children's factory labour in its present form. Combination of education with industrial production, etc.

When, in the course of development, class distinctions have disappeared, and all production has been concentrated in the hands of a vast association of the whole nation, the public power will lose its political character. Political power, properly so called, is merely the organized power of one class for oppressing another. If the proletariat during its contest with the bourgeoisie is compelled, by the force of circumstances, to organize itself as a class; if, by means of a revolution, it makes itself the ruling class, and, as such, sweeps away by force the old conditions of production, then it will, along with these conditions, have swept away the conditions for the existence of class antagonisms and of classes generally, and will thereby have abolished its own supremacy as a class.

In place of the old bourgeois society, with its classes and class antagonisms, we shall have an association, in which the free development of each is the condition for the free development of all.

III. Socialist and Communist Literature

1. Reactionary Socialism

a. Feudal Socialism. Owing to their historical position, it became the vocation of the aristocracies of France and England to write pamphlets against modern bourgeois society. In the French revolution of July 1830, and in the English Reform agitation,[10] these aristocracies again succumbed to the hateful upstart. Thenceforth, a serious political contest was altogether out of the question. A literary battle alone remained possible. But even in the domain of literature the old cries of the Restoration period[11] had become impossible.

---

10   Of 1830-1832.
11   Not the English Restoration 1660-1689, but the French Restoration 1814-1830 [Engels].

In order to arouse sympathy, the aristocracy were obliged to lose sight, apparently, of their own interests, and to formulate their indictment against the bourgeoisie in the interest of the exploited working class alone. Thus the aristocracy took their revenge by singing lampoons on their new master, and whispering in his ears sinister prophecies of coming catastrophe.

In this way arose feudal socialism: half lamentation, half lampoon; half echo of the past, half menace of the future; at times, by its bitter, witty and incisive criticism, striking the bourgeoisie to the very heart's core; but always ludicrous in its effect, through total incapacity to comprehend the march of modern history.

The aristocracy, in order to rally the people to them, waved the proletarian alms-bag in front for a banner. But the people, so often as it joined them, saw on their hindquarters the old feudal coats of arms, and deserted with loud and irreverent laughter.

One section of the French Legitimists,[12] and 'Young England',[13] exhibited this spectacle.

In pointing out that their mode of exploitation was different to that of the bourgeoisie, the feudalists forget that they exploited under circumstances and conditions that were quite different, and that are now antiquated. In showing that, under their rule, the modern proletariat never existed, they forget that the modern bourgeoisie is the necessary offspring of their own form of society.

For the rest, so little do they conceal the reactionary character of their criticism that their chief accusation against the bourgeoisie amounts to this, that under the bourgeois regime a class is being developed, which is destined to cut up root and branch the old order of society.

What they upbraid the bourgeoisie with is

---

12 The supporters of the restored Bourbon monarchy of 1814-1830, representing the landed aristocracy.

13 A literary circle attached to the Tory party. Benjamin Disraeli's *Sybil: or The Two Nations*, and Thomas Carlyle's pamphlets, were among its typical expressions.

not so much that it creates a proletariat, as that it creates a *revolutionary* proletariat.

In political practice, therefore, they join in all coercive measures against the working class; and in ordinary life, despite their highfalutin phrases, they stoop to pick up the golden apples dropped from the tree of industry, and to barter truth, love, and honour for traffic in wool, beetroot-sugar, and potato spirits.[14]

As the parson has ever gone hand in hand with the landlord, so has clerical socialism with feudal socialism.

Nothing is easier than to give Christian asceticism a socialist tinge. Has not Christianity declaimed against private property, against

---

14 This applies chiefly to Germany where the landed aristocracy and squirearchy have large portions of their estates cultivated for their own account by stewards, and are, moreover, extensive beetroot-sugar manufacturers and distillers of potato spirits. The wealthier British aristocracy are, as yet, rather above that; but they, too, know how to make up for declining rents by lending their names to floaters of more or less shady joint-stock companies [Engels].

marriage, against the state? Has it not preached in the place of these, charity and poverty, celibacy and mortification of the flesh, monastic life and Mother Church? Christian socialism is but the holy water with which the priest consecrates the heart-burnings of the aristocrat.

b. Petty-Bourgeois Socialism. The feudal aristocracy was not the only class that was ruined by the bourgeoisie, not the only class whose conditions of existence pined and perished in the atmosphere of modern bourgeois society. The medieval burgesses and the small peasant proprietors were the precursors of the modern bourgeoisie. In those countries which are but little developed, industrially and commercially, these two classes still vegetate side by side with the rising bourgeoisie.

In countries where modern civilization has become fully developed, a new class of petty bourgeois has been formed, fluctuating between proletariat and bourgeoisie and ever renewing itself as a supplementary part of bourgeois society. The individual members of this class, however, are being constantly hurled down into the proletariat by the action of competition, and, as modern industry develops, they even see the moment approaching when they will completely disappear as an independent section of modern society, to be replaced, in manufacture, agriculture and commerce, by overseers, bailiffs, and shop assistants.

In countries like France, where the peasants constitute far more than half of the population, it was natural that writers who sided with the proletariat against the bourgeoisie should use, in their criticism of the bourgeois regime, the standard of the peasant and petty bourgeois, and from the standpoint of these intermediate classes should take up the cudgels for the working class. Thus arose petty-bourgeois socialism. Sismondi[15] was the head of this school, not only in France but also in England.

---

15 Sismondi's *Principles of Political Economy* first appeared in 1803.

This school of socialism dissected with great acuteness the contradictions in the conditions of modern production. It laid bare the hypocritical apologies of economists. It proved, incontrovertibly, the disastrous effects of machinery and division of labour; the concentration of capital and land in a few hands; overproduction and crises; it pointed out the inevitable ruin of the petty bourgeois and peasant, the misery of the proletariat, the anarchy in production, the crying inequalities in the distribution of wealth, the industrial war of extermination between nations, the dissolution of old moral bonds, of the old family relations, of the old nationalities.

In its positive aims, however, this form of socialism aspires either to restoring the old means of production and of exchange, and with them the old property relations and the old society, or to cramping the modern means of production and of exchange within the framework of the old property relations that have been, and were bound to be, exploded by those means. In either case, it is both reactionary and utopian.

Its last words are: corporate guilds for manufacture; patriarchal relations in agriculture.

Ultimately, when stubborn historical facts had dispersed all intoxicating effects of self-deception, this form of socialism ended in a miserable fit of the blues.

c. German or 'True' Socialism. The socialist and communist literature of France, a literature that originated under the pressure of a bourgeoisie in power, and that was the expression of the struggle against this power, was introduced into Germany at a time when the bourgeoisie, in that country, had just begun its contest with feudal absolutism.

German philosophers, would-be philosophers and *beaux esprits* eagerly seized on this literature, only forgetting that when these writings immigrated from France into Germany, French social conditions had not immigrated along with them. In contact with German social conditions, this French literature lost all its immediate practical significance, and assumed a purely literary aspect.[16] Thus, to the German philosophers of the eighteenth century, the demands of the first French revolution were nothing more than the demands of 'practical reason' in general, and the utterance of the will of the revolutionary French bourgeoisie signified in their eyes the laws of pure will, of will as it was bound to be, of true human will generally.

The work of the German *literati* consisted solely in bringing the new French ideas into harmony with their ancient philosophical conscience, or rather, in annexing the French ideas without deserting their own philosophic point of view.

This annexation took place in the same way in which a foreign language is appropriated, namely by translation.

It is well known how the monks wrote silly lives of Catholic saints *over* the manuscripts on

---

16   In the German editions of the *Manifesto* there is an additional sentence here which reads (1872): 'It was bound to appear as idle speculation about the realization of the essence of man.'

which the classical works of ancient heathendom had been written. The German *literati* reversed this process with the profane French literature. They wrote their philosophical nonsense beneath the French original. For instance, beneath the French criticism of the economic functions of money, they wrote 'alienation of humanity', and beneath the French criticism of the bourgeois state they wrote, 'dethronement of the category of the general', and so forth.

The introduction of these philosophical phrases at the back of the French historical criticisms they dubbed 'philosophy of action', 'true socialism', 'German science of socialism', 'philosophical foundation of socialism', and so on.

The French socialist and communist literature was thus completely emasculated. And, since it ceased in the hands of the German to express the struggle of one class with the other, he felt conscious of having overcome 'French one-sidedness' and of representing, not true requirements, but the requirements of truth; not the interests of the proletariat, but the interests of human nature, of man in general, who belongs to no class, has no reality, who exists only in the misty realm of philosophical fantasy.

This German socialism, which took its school-boy task so seriously and solemnly, and extolled its poor stock-in-trade in such mountebank fashion, meanwhile gradually lost its pedantic innocence.

The fight of the German, and especially the Prussian bourgeoisie, against feudal aristocracy and absolute monarchy, in other words, the liberal movement, became more earnest.

By this, the long wished-for opportunity was offered to 'true' socialism of confronting the political movement with the socialist demands, of hurling the traditional anathemas against liberalism, against representative government, against bourgeois competition, bourgeois freedom of the press, bourgeois legislation, bourgeois liberty and equality, and of preaching to the masses that they had nothing to gain, and everything to lose, by this bourgeois movement. German socialism forgot, in the nick of time, that the French criticism, whose silly echo it was, presupposed the existence of modern bourgeois society, with its corresponding economic conditions of existence and the political constitution adapted thereto, the very things whose attainment was the object of the pending struggle in Germany.

To the absolute governments, with their following of parsons, professors, country squires and officials, it served as a welcome scarecrow against the threatening bourgeoisie.

It was a sweet finish after the bitter pills of floggings and bullets with which these same governments, just at that time, dosed the German working-class risings.[17]

While this 'true' socialism thus served the governments as a weapon for fighting the German bourgeoisie, it, at the same time, directly represented a reactionary interest, the interest of the German philistines. In Germany the petty-bourgeois class, a relic of the sixteenth century, and since then constantly cropping up again under various forms, is the real social basis of the existing state of things.

17   That is, the Silesian weavers' revolt of 1844.

To preserve this class is to preserve the existing state of things in Germany. The industrial and political supremacy of the bourgeoisie threatens it with certain destruction—on the one hand, from the concentration of capital; on the other, from the rise of a revolutionary proletariat. 'True' socialism appeared to kill these two birds with one stone. It spread like an epidemic.

The robe of speculative cobwebs, embroidered with flowers of rhetoric, steeped in the dew of sickly sentiment, this transcendental robe in which the German socialists wrapped their sorry 'eternal truths', all skin and bone, served to wonderfully increase the sale of their goods amongst such a public.

And on its part, German socialism recognized, more and more, its own calling as the bombastic representative of the petty-bourgeois philistine.

It proclaimed the German nation to be the model nation, and the German petty philistine to be the typical man. To every villainous meanness of this model man it gave a hidden, higher, socialistic interpretation, the exact contrary of its real character. It went to the extreme length of directly opposing the 'brutally destructive' tendency of communism, and of proclaiming its supreme and impartial contempt of all class struggles. With very few exceptions, all the so-called socialist and communist publications that now (1847) circulate in Germany belong to the domain of this foul and enervating literature.

2. Conservative or Bourgeois Socialism

A part of the bourgeoisie is desirous of redressing social grievances, in order to secure the continued existence of bourgeois society.

To this section belong economists, philanthropists, humanitarians, improvers of the condition of the working class, organizers of charity, members of societies for the prevention of cruelty to animals, temperance fanatics, hole-and-corner reformers of every imaginable kind. This form of socialism has, moreover, been worked out into complete systems.

We may cite Proudhon's *Philosophie de la Misère*[18] as an example of this form.

The socialistic bourgeois want all the advantages of modern social conditions without the struggles and dangers necessarily resulting therefrom. They desire the existing state of society minus its revolutionary and disintegrating elements. They wish for a bourgeoisie without a proletariat. The bourgeoisie naturally conceives the world in which it is supreme to be the best; and bourgeois socialism develops this comfortable conception into various more or less complete systems. In requiring the proletariat to carry out such a system, and thereby to march straightway into the social New Jerusalem, it but requires in reality that the proletariat should remain within the bounds of existing society, but should cast away all its hateful ideas concerning the bourgeoisie.

A second and more practical, but less systematic, form of this socialism sought to depreciate

18   It was in reply to Proudhon's *Philosophy of Poverty* (1846) that Marx wrote his *Poverty of Philosophy* (1847).

every revolutionary movement in the eyes of the working class, by showing that no mere political reform, but only a change in the material conditions of existence, in economical relations, could be of any advantage to them. By changes in the material conditions of existence, this form of socialism, however, by no means understands abolition of the bourgeois relations of production, an abolition that can be effected only by a revolution, but administrative reforms, based on the continued existence of these relations; reforms, therefore, that in no respect affect the relations between capital and labour, but, at the best, lessen the cost, and simplify the administrative work, of bourgeois government.

Bourgeois socialism attains adequate expression when, and only when, it becomes a mere figure of speech.

Free trade: for the benefit of the working class. Protective duties: for the benefit of the working class. Prison reform: for the benefit of the working class. This is the last word and the only seriously meant word of bourgeois socialism.

It is summed up in the phrase: the bourgeois is a bourgeois—for the benefit of the working class.

3. Critical-Utopian Socialism and Communism

We do not here refer to that literature which, in every great modern revolution, has always given voice to the demands of the proletariat, such as the writings of Babeuf and others.

The first direct attempts of the proletariat to attain its own ends, made in times of universal excitement, when feudal society was being over-thrown, these attempts necessarily failed, owing to the then undeveloped state of the proletar-iat, as well as to the absence of the economic conditions for its emancipation, conditions that had yet to be produced, and could be produced by the impending bourgeois epoch alone. The revolutionary literature that accompanied these first movements of the proletariat had necessar-ily a reactionary character. It inculcated univer-sal asceticism and social levelling in its crudest form.

The socialist and communist systems properly so called, those of Saint-Simon, Fourier, Owen and others, spring into existence in the early undeveloped period, described above, of the struggle between proletariat and bourgeoisie (see section I, 'Bourgeois and Proletarians').

The founders of these systems see, indeed, the class antagonisms, as well as the action of the decomposing elements in the prevailing form of society. But the proletariat, as yet in its infancy, offers to them the spectacle of a class without any historical initiative or any independent political movement.

Since the development of class antagonism keeps even pace with the development of industry, the economic situation, as they find it, does not as yet offer to them the material conditions for the emancipation of the proletariat. They therefore search after a new social science,[19]

---

19 Here, as in other writings of the 1840s, Marx and Engels still used 'science' in a now archaic sense of the term, roughly equivalent to the modern 'doctrine'. Although the substance of their argument remained the

after new social laws, that are to create these conditions.

Historical action is to yield to their personal inventive action, historically created conditions of emancipation to fantastic ones, and the gradual, spontaneous class organization of the proletariat to an organization of society specially contrived by these inventors. Future history resolves itself, in their eyes, into the propaganda and the practical carrying out of their social plans.

In the formation of their plans they are conscious of caring chiefly for the interests of the working class, as being the most suffering class. Only from the point of view of being the most suffering class does the proletariat exist for them.

The undeveloped state of the class struggle, as well as their own surroundings, cause socialists

---

same, the change in usage led them later to refer to their own theory as 'scientific', in contrast to the utopianism of their predecessors. See, for example, Marx's Preface to the first German edition of *Capital*, and Engels's 'Socialism: Utopian and Scientific', both in Marx–Engels, *Selected Works*, Lawrence & Wishart (London 1968).

of this kind to consider themselves far superior to all class antagonisms. They want to improve the condition of every member of society, even that of the most favoured. Hence, they habitually appeal to society at large, without distinction of class; nay, by preference, to the ruling class. For how can people, when once they understand their system, fail to see in it the best possible plan of the best possible state of society?

Hence, they reject all political, and especially all revolutionary, action; they wish to attain their ends by peaceful means, and endeavour, by small experiments, necessarily doomed to failure, and by the force of example, to pave the way for the new social gospel.

Such fantastic pictures of future society, painted at a time when the proletariat is still in a very undeveloped state and has but a fantastic conception of its own position, correspond with the first instinctive yearnings of that class for a general reconstruction of society.

But these socialist and communist publications contain also a critical element. They attack every principle of existing society. Hence they are full of the most valuable materials for the enlightenment of the working class. The practical measures proposed in them—such as the abolition of the distinction between town and country, of the family, of the carrying on of industries for the account of private individuals, and of the wage system, the proclamation of social harmony, the conversion of the functions of the state into a mere superintendence of production—all these proposals point solely to the disappearance of class antagonisms which were, at the time, only just cropping up, and which, in these publications, are recognized under their earliest, indistinct and undefined forms only. These proposals, therefore, are of a purely utopian character.

The significance of critical–utopian socialism and communism bears an inverse relation to historical development. In proportion as the modern class struggle develops and takes definite shape, this fantastic standing apart from the contest, these fantastic attacks on it, lose all practical value and all theoretical justification. Therefore, although the originators of these systems were, in many respects, revolutionary, their disciples have, in every case, formed mere reactionary sects. They hold fast by the original views of their masters, in opposition to the progressive historical development of the proletariat. They therefore endeavour, and that consistently, to deaden the class struggle and to reconcile the class antagonisms. They still dream of experimental realization of their social utopias, of founding isolated '*phalanstères*', of establishing 'home colonies', of setting up a 'little Icaria'[20]—duodecimo editions of the New Jerusalem—and to realize all these castles in the air, they are compelled to appeal to the feelings and purses of the bourgeois. By degrees they sink into the category of the reactionary conservative socialists depicted above, differing from these only by more systematic pedantry, and by their fanatical and superstitious

---

20   *Phalanstères* were socialist colonies on the plan of Charles Fourier; Icaria was the name given by Cabet to his utopia and, later on, to his American communist colony [Engels].

belief in the miraculous effects of their social science.

They therefore violently oppose all political action on the part of the working class; such action, according to them, can only result from blind unbelief in the new gospel.

The Owenites in England, and the Fourierists in France, respectively oppose the Chartists and the Réformistes.

IV. Position of the Communists in Relation to the Various Existing Opposition Parties

Section II has made clear the relations of the Communists to the existing working-class parties, such as the Chartists in England and the agrarian reformers[21] in America.

The Communists fight for the attainment of the immediate aims, for the enforcement of the

---

21 This seems to be reference to the Free Soil movement, which demanded the free distribution of uncultivated land to small farmers.

momentary interests of the working class; but in the movement of the present, they also represent and take care of the future of that movement. In France the Communists ally themselves with the Social-Democrats,[22] against the conservative and radical bourgeoisie, reserving, however, the right to take up a critical position in regard to phrases and illusions traditionally handed down from the great Revolution.

In Switzerland they support the Radicals, without losing sight of the fact that this party consists of antagonistic elements, partly of democratic socialists, in the French sense, partly of radical bourgeois.

In Poland they support the party that insists on an agrarian revolution as the prime condition for national emancipation, that party which fomented the insurrection of Cracow in 1846.

---

22   The party then represented in parliament by Ledru-Rollin, in literature by Louis Blanc, in the daily press by *La Réforme*. The name 'Social-Democracy' signified, with these its inventors, a section of the democratic or republican party more or less tinged with socialism [Engels].

In Germany they fight with the bourgeoisie whenever it acts in a revolutionary way, against the absolute monarchy, the feudal squirearchy, and the petty bourgeoisie.[23]

But they never cease, for a single instant, to instil into the working class the clearest possible recognition of the hostile antagonism between bourgeoisie and proletariat, in order that the German workers may straightway use, as so many weapons against the bourgeoisie, the social and political conditions that the bourgeoisie must necessarily introduce along with its supremacy, and in order that, after the fall of the reactionary classes in Germany, the fight against the bourgeoisie itself may immediately begin.

The Communists turn their attention chiefly to Germany, because that country is on the eve of a bourgeois revolution that is bound to be carried out under more advanced conditions of European civilization, and with a much more developed proletariat, than that of England was

---

23 *Kleinbürgerei* in the original. 'Petty-bourgeois conditions' would be a more accurate translation.

in the seventeenth, and of France in the eighteenth century, and because the bourgeois revolution in Germany will be but the prelude to an immediately following proletarian revolution.

In short, the Communists everywhere support every revolutionary movement against the existing social and political order of things.

In all these movements they bring to the front, as the leading question in each, the property question, no matter what its degree of development at the time.

Finally, they labour everywhere for the union and agreement of the democratic parties of all countries.

The Communists disdain to conceal their views and aims. They openly declare that their ends can be attained only by the forcible overthrow of all existing conditions. Let the ruling classes tremble at a communistic revolution. The proletarians have nothing to lose but their chains. They have a world to win.

WORKING MEN OF ALL COUNTRIES, UNITE!

Preface to the English Edition of 1888[1]

Friedrich Engels

The *Manifesto* was published as the platform of the Communist League, a working men's association, first exclusively German, later on international, and, under the political conditions of the Continent before 1848, unavoidably a secret society. At a congress of the League, held in London in November 1847,

---

1 The preceding translation of the *Communist Manifesto* was made by Samuel Moore in 1888, and edited by Engels. His notes are identified in this edition by [Engels]. Besides printer's errors, inconsistent and old-fashioned punctuation and orthography, a very few linguistic archaisms have also been amended.

Marx and Engels were commissioned to prepare for publication a complete theoretical and practical party programme. Drawn up in German, in January 1848, the manuscript was sent to the printer in London a few weeks before the French revolution of 24 February. A French translation was brought out in Paris shortly before the insurrection of June 1848. The first English translation, by Miss Helen Macfarlane, appeared in George Julian Harney's *Red Republican*, London, 1850. A Danish and a Polish edition had also been published.

The defeat of the Parisian insurrection of June 1848—the first great battle between proletariat and bourgeoisie—drove again into the background, for a time, the social and political aspirations of the European working class. Thenceforth, the struggle for supremacy was again, as it had been before the revolution of February, solely between different sections of the propertied class; the working class was reduced to a fight for political elbow-room, and to the position of extreme wing of the middle-class radicals.

Wherever independent proletarian movements continued to show signs of life, they were ruthlessly hunted down. Thus the Prussian police hunted out the Central Board[2] of the Communist League, then located in Cologne. The members were arrested, and, after eighteen months' imprisonment, they were tried in October 1852. This celebrated 'Cologne Communist Trial' lasted from 4 October till 12 November; seven of the prisoners were sentenced to terms of imprisonment in a fortress, varying from three to six years. Immediately after the sentence, the League was formally dissolved by the remaining members. As to the *Manifesto*, it seemed thenceforth to be doomed to oblivion.

When the European working class had recovered sufficient strength for another attack on the ruling classes, the International Working Men's Association sprang up. But this association, formed with the express aim of welding into one body the whole militant proletariat of Europe

---

2 That is, the Central Committee, as it is referred to elsewhere.

and America, could not at once proclaim the principles laid down in the *Manifesto*. The International was bound to have a programme broad enough to be acceptable to the English trade unions, to the followers of Proudhon in France, Belgium, Italy and Spain, and to the Lassalleans[3] in Germany. Marx, who drew up this programme to the satisfaction of all parties, entirely trusted to the intellectual development of the working class, which was sure to result from combined action and mutual discussion. The very events and vicissitudes of the struggle against capital, the defeats even more than the victories, could not help bringing home to men's minds the insufficiency of their various favourite nostrums, and preparing the way for a more complete insight into the true conditions of working-class emancipation. And Marx was right. The International,

---

3 Lassalle personally, to us, always acknowledged himself to be a disciple of Marx, and, as such, stood on the ground of the *Manifesto*. But in his public agitation, 1862-1864, he did not go beyond demanding cooperative workshops supported by state credit [Engels].

on its breaking up in 1874,[4] left the workers quite different men from what it had found them in 1864. Proudhonism in France, Lassalleanism in Germany were dying out, and even the conservative English trade unions, though most of them had long since severed their connection with the International, were gradually advancing towards that point at which, last year at Swansea, their President could say in their name, 'Continental socialism has lost its terrors for us.'[5] In fact: the principles of the *Manifesto* had made considerable headway among the working men of all countries.

The *Manifesto* itself thus came to the front again. The German text had been, since 1850, reprinted several times in Switzerland, England and America. In 1872, it was translated into English in New York, where the translation was

---

4   In fact the International was not officially wound up until 1876, although it effectively ceased to function when the General Council was transferred to New York in 1872.

5   W. Bevan, in his address to the TUC Congress, reported in the *Commonweal*, 17 September 1887.

published in *Woodhull and Claflin's Weekly*.[6] From this English version, a French one was made in *Le Socialiste* of New York. Since then at least two more English translations, more or less mutilated, have been brought out in America, and one of them has been reprinted in England. The first Russian translation, made by Bakunin, was published at Herzen's *Kolokol*[7] office in Geneva, about 1863; a second one, by the heroic Vera Zasulich,[8] also in Geneva, 1882. A new Danish

---

6   This paper was published by two American feminists, Victoria Woodhull and her sister Tennessee Claflin, whose campaign Marx considered 'middle-class humbug' and who were eventually expelled from the International. See International Working Men's Association, *Documents of the First International*, Lawrence & Wishart (London 1964-1966), pp. 223-32. It carried an abridged translation of the *Manifesto* on 30 December 1871.

7   Alexander Herzen was a Russian philosopher and revolutionary democrat. His paper *Kolokol* (The Bell) was the leading organ of the Russian emigration in the 1860s. Bakunin's translation of the *Manifesto* was in fact published in 1869.

8   Engels celebrates Vera Zasulich for her attempted assassination of the governor of St Petersburg, General

edition is to be found in *Socialdemokratisk Bibliothek*, Copenhagen, 1885; a fresh French translation in *Le Socialiste*, Paris, 1885. From this latter a Spanish version was prepared and published in Madrid, 1886. The German reprints are not to be counted, there have been twelve altogether at the least. An Armenian translation, which was to be published in Constantinople some months ago, did not see the light, I am told, because the publisher was afraid of bringing out a book with the name of Marx on it, while the translator declined to call it his own production. Of further translations into other languages I have heard, but have not seen them. Thus the history of the *Manifesto* reflects, to a great extent, the history of the modern working-class movement; at present it is undoubtedly the most widespread, the most international production of all socialist literature, the common platform acknowledged by millions of working men from Siberia to California.

Trepov, in 1878. The translation was in fact by George Plekhanov, the founder of Russian Marxism.

Yet, when it was written, we could not have called it a 'Socialist' manifesto. By 'socialists', in 1847, were understood, on the one hand, the adherents of the various utopian systems: Owenites in England, Fourierists in France, both of them already reduced to the position of mere sects, and gradually dying out; on the other hand, the most multifarious social quacks, who, by all manners of tinkering, professed to redress, without any danger to capital and profit, all sorts of social grievances; in both cases men outside the working-class movement, and looking rather to the 'educated' classes for support. Whatever portion of the working class had become convinced of the insufficiency of mere political revolutions, and had proclaimed the necessity of a total social change, that portion then called itself Communist. It was a crude, rough-hewn, purely instinctive sort of communism; still, it touched the cardinal point and was powerful enough amongst the working class to produce the utopian communism, in France, of Cabet, and in Germany, of Weitling. Thus, socialism was, in 1847, a middle-class movement, communism a working-class movement. Socialism was, on the Continent at least, 'respectable'; communism was the very opposite. And as our notion, from the very beginning, was that 'the emancipation of the working class must be the act of the working class itself', there could be no doubt as to which of the two names we must take. Moreover, we have, ever since, been far from repudiating it.

The *Manifesto* being our joint production, I consider myself bound to state that the fundamental proposition, which forms its nucleus, belongs to Marx. That proposition is: that in every historical epoch, the prevailing mode of economic production and exchange, and the social organization necessarily following from it, form the basis upon which is built up, and from which alone can be explained, the political and intellectual history of that epoch; that consequently the whole history of mankind (since the dissolution of primitive tribal society, holding land in common ownership) has been a history of class struggles, contests between exploiting and exploited, ruling and oppressed classes; that the history of these class struggles forms a series of evolutions in which, nowadays, a stage has been reached where the exploited and oppressed class—the proletariat—cannot attain its emancipation from the sway of the exploiting and ruling class—the bourgeoisie—without, at the same time, and once and for all, emancipating society at large from all exploitation, oppression, class distinctions and class struggles.

This proposition which, in my opinion, is destined to do for history what Darwin's theory has done for biology, we, both of us, had been gradually approaching for some years before 1845. How far I had independently progressed towards it is best shown by my *Condition of the Working Class in England*. But when I again met Marx at Brussels, in spring 1845, he had it already worked out, and put it before me, in terms almost as clear as those in which I have stated it here.

From our joint preface to the German edition of 1872, I quote the following:

However much the state of things may have altered during the last twenty-five years, the general principles laid down in this *Manifesto* are, on the whole, as correct today as ever. Here and there some detail might be improved. The practical application of the principles will depend, as the *Manifesto* itself states, everywhere and at all times, on the historical conditions for the time being existing, and, for that reason, no special stress is laid on the revolutionary measures proposed at the end of section II. That passage would, in many respects, be very differently worded today. In view of the gigantic strides of modern industry since 1848, and of the accompanying improved and extended organization of the working class; in view of the practical experience gained, first in the February revolution, and then, still more, in the Paris Commune, where the proletariat for the first time held political power for two whole months, this programme has in some details become antiquated. One thing especially was proved by the Commune, viz., that 'the working class cannot simply lay hold of the ready-made state machinery, and wield it for its own purposes'. (See 'The Civil War in France', section III, where this point is further developed.) Further, it is self-evident that the criticism of socialist literature is deficient in relation to the present time, because it comes down only to 1847; also, that the remarks on the relation of the Communists to the various opposition parties (section IV), although in principle still correct, yet in practice are antiquated, because the political situation has been entirely changed, and the progress of history has swept from off the earth the greater portion of the political parties there enumerated.

But then, the *Manifesto* has become a historical document which we have no longer any right to alter.

The present translation is by Mr Samuel Moore, the translator of the greater portion of Marx's *Capital*. We have revised it in common, and I have added a few notes explanatory of historical allusions.

London
30 January 1888

Introduction to
the April Theses

Tariq Ali

Marxist ideas penetrated and spread in Tsarist Russia much sooner than they ever did in Britain, where the *Communist Manifesto* was first published and where *Capital* was composed in its entirety. The impact was much greater in St Petersburg and Moscow than in London or Manchester. A few decades later, Lenin would confront this contradiction between theory and practice and provide the political–theoretical basis for transcending it on a global scale. He argued that the development of capitalism and its degenerate extension, imperialism, had destroyed all the progressive capacities it had displayed in its youth during the battles against absolutist feudalism. It was now an oppressor, subjugating the world in its own narrow interests:

> The first epoch from the great French revolution to the Franco-Prussian war is one of the rise of the bourgeoisie, of its triumph, of the bourgeoisie on the upgrade, an epoch of bourgeois–democratic movements in general and of bourgeois–national movements in particular, an epoch of the rapid breakdown of the obsolete feudal–absolutist institution. The second epoch is that of the full domination and decline of the bourgeoisie, one of transition from its progressive character towards reactionary and even ultra-reactionary finance capital.[1]

---

1 V. I. Lenin, *Collected Works,* Vol. 21 (Moscow 1975), p. 146.

The third epoch that had set in was, he argued, a crucial one because it 'places the bourgeoisie in the same "position" as that in which the feudal lords found themselves during the first epoch. This is the epoch of imperialism and imperialist upheavals'; the logic for him was now obvious. An all-out battle between the global oppression of capital and its victims with tactics developed according to location and need.

Lenin's contention that the chain breaks at its weakest link first was proved correct but the other capitalist links in Western Europe and the United States (and later in Asia and South America) welded themselves back together, survived and grew stronger. The weakest link of the capitalist chain, during his lifetime, turned out to be the most backward imperial state in Europe, Tsarist Russia; the strongest, its most advanced industrialized counterpart, Britain. Germany lay somewhere in between. Marx's writings did not offer too much hope to the small, if growing, industrial proletariat in Russia. He had virtually declared a revolution in Russia to be theoretically impossible. Later, he did mention in passing the possibility of the Russian peasant commune serving as a red base, but these were essentially throwaway lines designed not to discourage his Russian followers too much.

The February Revolution that toppled the Tsar in 1917 took Lenin and all the exiled revolutionaries by surprise. The idea of approaching the Germans for a special train back home came from the Left–Menshevik leader, Julius Martov, and even though he refused to board it till the representative council (the Soviet) in Petrograd approved the decision, the others were less fussy. It was vital they got back as soon as possible. Accepting opportunist German help was not too big a deal since a revolution was bound to break out in that country as well. Kaiser Wilhelm argued the opposite. Help them if we must if it shortens the war, he told his senior civil servants, but once we take Russia we'll destroy these Bolsheviks like vermin. The Bolsheviks were banking on a German revolution to take care of that problem.

They had, after all, opposed the barbarism of the First World War. Lenin, isolated yet again at the Zimmerwald anti-war conference in 1917, had insisted the only credible goal was to turn the imperialist war into a civil war. The enemy was at home. Another manifestation of Jacobin voluntarism, his opponents had mocked. Will this fellow never learn? But this fellow was being vindicated by history, whose pace had been quickened by the war. Even Lenin had not imagined that the war would disintegrate the Tsarist Empire at such a speed. It was not a workers' uprising, but (even more than in 1905 after the defeat inflicted by the Japanese) the growing realization that the war, as far as Russia was concerned, could not be won. Desertions, food shortages, the use of the uniformed peasants as cannon fodder were all beginning to divide the Tsarist armies. The peasants in uniform killing and being killed on the battlefields of the First World War were being radicalized.

The three texts by Lenin were written between the outbreak of the revolution in February 1917 and its completion in November that same year. Alexander Herzen had insisted the 'dialectic was the algebra of revolution'. It was a clunky phrase but accurate. What was the way out of the contradiction? How could it be resolved? Lenin became obsessed with these questions. His answer was to stress the primacy of politics, of revolutionary strategy and tactics, above economics and sociology. All these ideas had taken shape in *What Is to Be Done?*, his pamphlet of 1902, which a year later permanently divided the Russian Social Democratic Party. Spontaneity, argued Lenin, would never be enough. Trade-unionism, by its very nature, was addicted to the status quo. Its dialectic of partial conquests—if we ask for more we might lose what we have already won—made it a defensive, conservative and insufficient force. In any case, the Russian proletariat was too small and too weak economically and socially to spark off a revolution on its own. The peasantry was not an undifferentiated and inert mass. It represented the majority of the population and had to be won over, encouraged to break the chains of its oppression and united with other forces to assault the citadels of Tsarist power. Radical politics required a radical instrument: a revolutionary political party. These ideas led to the usual charges of sectarianism, utopianism, voluntarism, Jacobinism.

Since the outbreak of the revolution, Lenin had diverted his own activities. No more lectures. No more café discussions. His main task, he told Alexandra Kollontai, was composing a daily essay for *Pravda* now that it was legal. The press had become a crucial conveyor belt. In his first 'Letter from Afar' he explained to Russian readers from Zurich why what had happened was no 'miracle' as conservative leaders were suggesting, but the beginning of a new epoch, one of wars and revolutions:

> The first revolution engendered by the imperialist world war has broken out. The first revolution, but certainly not the last. Judging by the scanty information available in Switzerland … The first stage of our revolution will certainly not be the

last … There are no miracles in nature or history, but every abrupt turn in history, and this applies to every revolution, presents such a wealth of content, unfolds such unexpected and specific combinations of forms of struggle and alignment of forces of the contestants, that to the lay mind there is much that appears miraculous … The combination of a number of factors of world historic importance was required for the tsarist monarchy to have collapsed in a few days … the all-powerful 'stage manager', this mighty accelerator, was the imperialist world war.

On the sealed train taking the exiles back to Russia, Lenin was buried in deep thought. Eyewitness reports agree he did not speak much, and even his habitual jottings were greatly reduced. He was thinking of the possibilities that now lay before the clandestine party he had painstakingly constructed over the past two decades. Its cadres, full-time revolutionaries in the main, would be the only force prepared to push the revolution forward. The internal party was now legal, its newspaper was being published and read by thousands, its leaders had been released and were awaiting him in Petrograd. Peasant consciousness was being altered by the war, and its impact in the Russian countryside was disastrous. His thoughts kept going back to Marx's writings on the state and its apparatuses. He knew well the essays—*The Eighteenth Brumaire* and *The Civil War in France*—in which the founding father of the movement had written of the need to confront the old state and create a new one: the commune–state.

By the time trains had been changed at Stockholm and Bolsheviks had joined Lenin's group, providing first-hand reports of what was actually going on, when they were on track to reach the Finland station in Petrograd, Lenin was much clearer in his conception of the revolution. His younger colleague Nikolai Bukharin had already come up with the slogan 'Smash the Bourgeois State', and Lenin pondered adopting it. But it was Marx's text that finally persuaded him. The political model was the Paris Commune, and backward Russia had produced the organs of direct democracy in the shape of the soviets. These should form the basis of alternative state structures on every level. The commune–state was the only possible replacement for the bourgeois state and the degenerate Tsarist monstrosity in Russia. For Lenin these were practical ideas, far removed from utopianism, and would be a much better gauge of mass consciousness and more democratic than any existing bourgeois assembly. All this would find its way to one of his most important texts, *The State and Revolution*.

He was working non-stop on a draft of something entitled 'The Tasks of the Proletariat in the Present Revolution' that would become known as 'The April Theses' and leave its mark on the twentieth century. Prior to Lenin no revolutionary leader or party had decided consciously on the road down which they were going to travel. Neither radicals to the left of Cromwell nor Robespierre and St Just had a map for the future. Toussaint L'Ouverture in Haiti and his black Jacobins wanted to abolish slavery and then wait and see. The Mexican leaders of the peasantry, Emiliano Zapata and Pancho Villa, did destroy the hacienda oligarchy but were outwitted and outmanoeuvred by gringos and a pro-gringo elite with disastrous consequences for the country. The demands of the Chinese leaders of the Boxer Rebellion were limited to sovereignty and Sun Yat-sen's republic was a brave, but doomed attempt to create a bourgeois democracy on the Western model.

In the first letters from Zurich he had more or less avoided the question. Was the February eruption a bourgeois democratic upheaval like the 1789 revolution in France? If, as Marxist orthodoxy and most of the present leaders of Russian social democracy insisted, the productive forces were seriously underdeveloped as they patently were in Russia, how long before they could make a socialist revolution? The theoreticians of German social democracy had been firm on this point; they had wanted their own 'tried and trusted methods' to be the model for all social-democratic parties. First build electoral strength via parliament, then obtain a majority and finally strike the enemy. But what of the enemy within the labour movement that had wreaked havoc in Germany, France, Britain and many smaller European states? Lenin had greatly respected Karl Kautsky, but once the German party, with honourable exceptions, had decided to back the imperialist world war and voted for war credits, all reverence was immediately discarded. This factor, often underestimated, played an extremely important part in Lenin's calculations. Relieved of the need to take the German party's advice seriously, he began to think afresh on what was to be done in Russia. What was the point of a bourgeois democratic revolution if all it did was retain power for the post-Tsarist oppressors, continue the war and ignore peasant and proletarian needs and demands? Perhaps what was needed was a combined revolution that pushed through all democratic demands as a prelude to something much more radical: a socialist revolution. Liberated Russia as a launch pad for the German revolution and others that would mark the beginning of the end for imperialism and its oppressed multi-continental colonies. He played with the idea of a 'revolutionary–democratic dictatorship of the proletariat and the poorest peasants' in opposition to the dictatorship of capital that ruled the imperialist countries but doubted whether this platypus could be brought into being.

After the dress rehearsal of 1905, Lenin had criticized the arguments advanced by a group of socialists led by Trotsky. They believed, Lenin riposted, 'that a Socialist (i.e. proletarian) revolution was possible, as if the productive forces of the country were sufficiently developed for such a revolution to take place'. Now, with the curtain up on the actual revolution, Lenin found himself moving in the same direction. 'The April Theses' shook the Bolshevik party to its core. Lenin had been raging against the latest issues of *Pravda* in which Kamenev and Stalin were expressing critical support for the Provisional Government of Alexander Kerensky. The Bolshevik leader demanded a clean break via a slogan that insisted on the removal of all the capitalist ministers. A demand whose popularity grew as the war continued and the government proved itself incapable on every front. Both in the Soviet where the Right had a majority and in government, the moderates were paralysed: 'dual powerlessness' was Trotsky's witty description of the existing state of affairs.

There was a huge crowd waiting for Lenin at the Finland station, including officials from the Soviet. He spoke above their heads to those others who had also assembled to greet him, to those soldiers, workers, students and a sprinkling of intellectuals, attached and detached, who had made February possible. But before he could speak, Cheikdze, the official leader of the delegation despatched by the Petrograd Soviet, issued a welcome and a warning:

Comrade Lenin … we welcome you to Russia. But—we think that the principal task of the revolutionary democracy is now the defence of the revolution from any encroachments either from

within or from without. We consider that what
this goal requires is not disunion, but the closing
of the democratic ranks. We hope you will pursue
these goals together with us.

Lenin was not in a mood for any of this and virtually ignored this delegation. He was impatient
to speak, stood there as though nothing taking
place had the slightest connection with him and
then, turning away from the official delegation
altogether, he made this 'reply':

Dear Comrades, soldiers, sailors, and workers! I
am happy to greet in your persons the victorious
Russian revolution, and greet you as the vanguard
of the worldwide proletarian army … The pirat-
ical imperialist war is the beginning of civil war
throughout Europe … The hour is not far distant
when at the call of our comrade, Karl Liebknecht
[who was still alive at the time], the peoples will
turn their arms against their own capitalist exploit-
ers … The worldwide Socialist revolution has
already dawned … Any day now the whole of

European capitalism may crash. The Russian revolution accomplished by you has prepared the way and opened a new epoch. Long live the worldwide Socialist revolution!

His words were uncompromising, but he had thought about them for several weeks. They reflected the ten theses that would be made public on 7 April 1917. Their reception was a mixture of bewilderment and shock on the part of quite a few Bolshevik leaders and, naturally, all other parties of the Left. The style of the theses was that of a machine gun burst, followed by a staccato drum roll. The last thesis made it clear that the battleground he had chosen was international: 'Renovation of the International. Initiative, an International against *social chauvinism*, against the *centre*.' It was Kautsky he had in mind and others too, who, despite pledges to the contrary at every international gathering of the Second International and universal agreement to deal with the impending imperialist war by a Europe-wide strike, had been unable to resist

the tide of nationalist chauvinism. The capitula-
tion was on a huge scale and split the workers'
movement for three-quarters of a century. Had
they opposed the war the SPD leaders would
undoubtedly have been imprisoned like Rosa
Luxemburg and her comrades, but they would
have survived the war intact and, perhaps, not
surrendered to their own capitalist elite when
the war ended and Germany became a republic.
Might a German socialist revolution then have
been more impressive and would more have been
achieved than the isolated and isolating adven-
ture of the *Spartakusbund*? And, if so, would not
that event have led to a very different conclusion in Russia? Lenin was forever haunted by the
scale of Kautsky's betrayal and, in due course, a
polemic emerged. The title, as was often the case
with Lenin, left little room for ambiguity: *The
Proletarian Revolution and the Renegade Kautsky.*
He was the master of understanding the dialectic of friend/enemy.[2] 'The April Theses' was his

2   I intend to develop this and related themes further
in *The Dilemmas of Lenin* (forthcoming 2017).

response to his old teachers in Germany. The workers and their allies had to struggle for power now and so it happened. Twelve years of struggle and defeats were compressed into a decisive day of action. Victory. In his 'Notes in Defence of the April Theses', Lenin stressed once again that the need was for a commune–state:

> We must ably, carefully, clear people's minds and lead the proletariat and poor peasants *forward*, away from 'dual power' *towards the full power* of the Soviets of Workers Deputies, and this is the commune in Marx's sense, in the sense of the experience of 1871.

The ideas of Marx and revolutionary France never left him, despite the civil war and accompanied setbacks that lay ahead, and he returned to them as he lay paralysed for the last two years of his life.

London
May 2016

The Tasks of the Proletariat in the Present Revolution ('The April Theses')

V. I. Lenin

I did not arrive in Petrograd until the night of 3 April, and therefore at the meeting on 4 April I could, of course, deliver the report on the tasks of the revolutionary proletariat only on my own behalf, and with reservations as to insufficient preparation.[1]

---

1 Published in *Pravda*, No. 26, for 7 April 1917, over the signature *N. Lenin*, this article contains Lenin's famous 'April Theses' read by him at two meetings held at the Tauride Palace on 4 (17) April 1917 (at a meeting of Bolsheviks and at a joint meeting of Bolshevik and Menshevik delegates to the All-Russia Conference of Soviets of Workers' and Soldiers' Deputies).

The only thing I could do to make things easier for myself—and for *honest* opponents—was to prepare the theses *in writing*. I read them out, and gave the text to Comrade Tsereteli. I read them *twice* very slowly: first at a meeting of Bolsheviks and then at a meeting of both Bolsheviks and Mensheviks. I publish these personal theses of mine with only the briefest explanatory notes, which were developed in far greater detail in the report.

Theses

(1) In our attitude towards the war, which under the now government of Lvov and Co. unquestionably remains on Russia's part a predatory imperialist war owing to the capitalist nature of that government, not the slightest concession to 'revolutionary defencism' is permissible.

The class-conscious proletariat can give its consent to a revolutionary war, which would really justify revolutionary defencism, only on condition: (a) that the power pass to the proletariat and the poorest sections of the peasants aligned with the proletariat; (b) that all annexations be renounced in deed and not in word; (c) that a complete break with all capitalist interests be effected in actual fact.

In view of the undoubted honesty of those broad sections of the mass believers in revolutionary defencism who accept the war only as a necessity, and not as a means of conquest, in view of the fact that they are being deceived by the bourgeoisie, it is necessary with particular thoroughness, persistence and patience to explain their error to them, to explain the inseparable connection existing between capital and the imperialist war, and to prove that without overthrowing capital *it is impossible* to end the war by a truly democratic peace, a peace not imposed by violence.

The most widespread campaign for this view must be organized in the army at the front.

Fraternization.

(2) The specific feature of the present situation in Russia is that the country is *passing* from the first stage of the revolution—which, owing to the insufficient class-consciousness and organization of the proletariat, placed power in the hands of the bourgeoisie—to its *second* stage, which must place power in the hands of the proletariat and the poorest sections of the peasants.

This transition is characterized, on the one hand, by a maximum of legally recognized rights (Russia is *now* the freest of all the belligerent countries in the world); on the other, by the absence of violence towards the masses, and, finally, by their unreasoning trust in the government of capitalists, those worst enemies of peace and socialism.

This peculiar situation demands of us an ability to adapt ourselves to the *special* conditions of Party work among unprecedentedly large masses of proletarians who have just awakened to political life.

(3) No support for the Provisional Government; the utter falsity of all its promises should be

made clear, particularly of those relating to the renunciation of annexations. Exposure in place of the impermissible, illusion-breeding 'demand' that *this* government, a government of capitalists, should cease to be an imperialist government.

(4) Recognition of the fact that in most of the Soviets of Workers' Deputies our Party is in a minority, so far a small minority, as against *a bloc of all* the petty-bourgeois opportunist elements, from the Popular Socialists and the Socialist-Revolutionaries down to the Organizing Committee[2] (Chkheidze,

---

2   Popular Socialists: members of the petty-bourgeois Labour Popular Socialist Party, which separated from the right wing of the Socialist-Revolutionary Party in 1906. Socialist-Revolutionaries (SRs): a petty-bourgeois party formed in Russia at the end of 1901 and beginning of 1902 through the amalgamation of various Narodnik groups and circles. The SRs, together with the Mensheviks and Cadets, were the mainstay of the counter-revolutionary Provisional Government of the bourgeoisie and landowners, and the leaders of the party (Kerensky, Avksentyev, Chernov) were members of that government. Organizing Committee (OC): set up in 1912 at the August conference of the liquidators. During World War I the OC justified

Tsereteli, etc.), Steklov, etc., etc., who have yielded to the influence of the bourgeoisie and spread that influence among the proletariat.

The masses must be made to see that the Soviets of Workers' Deputies are the *only possible* form of revolutionary government, and that therefore our task is, as long as *this* government yields to the influence of the bourgeoisie, to present a patient, systematic, and persistent *explanation* of the errors of their tactics, an explanation especially adapted to the practical needs of the masses.

As long as we are in the minority we carry on the work of criticizing and exposing errors, and at the same time we preach the necessity of transferring the entire state power to the Soviets of Workers' Deputies, so that the people may overcome their mistakes by experience.

(5) Not a parliamentary republic—to return to a parliamentary republic from the Soviets of Workers' Deputies would be a retrograde

the war on the part of Tsarism, and advocated the ideas of nationalism and chauvinism.

step—but a republic of Soviets of Workers', Agricultural Labourers' and Peasants' Deputies throughout the country, from top to bottom.

Abolition of the police, the army and the bureaucracy.[3]

The salaries of all officials, all of whom are elective and displaceable at any time, not to exceed the average wage of a competent worker.

(6) The weight of emphasis in the agrarian programme to be shifted to the Soviets of Agricultural Labourers' Deputies.

Confiscation of all landed estates.

Nationalization of *all* lands in the country, the land to be disposed of by the local Soviets of Agricultural Labourers' and Peasants' Deputies. The organization of separate Soviets of Deputies of Poor Peasants. The setting up of a model farm on each of the large estates (ranging in size from 100 to 300 dessiatines, according to local and other conditions, and to the decisions of the

---

3 *Lenin's note*: That is, the standing army to be replaced by the arming of the whole people.

local bodies) under the control of the Soviets of Agricultural Labourers' Deputies and for the public account.

(7) The immediate amalgamation of all banks in the country into a single national bank, and the institution of control over it by the Soviet of Workers' Deputies.

(8) It is not our *immediate* task to 'introduce' socialism, but only to bring social production and the distribution of products at once under the control of the Soviets of Workers' Deputies.

(9) Party tasks:
  (a) Immediate convocation of a Party congress;
  (b) Alteration of the Party Programme, mainly:
      (i) On the question of imperialism and the imperialist war;
      (ii) On our attitude towards the state and our demand for a 'commune state';[4]

---

4 *Lenin's note*: That is, a state of which the Paris Commune was the prototype.

(iii) Amendment of our out-of-date minimum programme.

(c) Change of the Party's name.[5]

(10) A new International.

We must take the initiative in creating a revolutionary International, an International against
the *social-chauvinists* and against the 'Centre'.[6]

In order that the reader may understand why
I had especially to emphasize as a rare exception the 'case' of honest opponents, I invite him
to compare the above theses with the following
objection by Mr Goldenberg: Lenin, he said, 'has

---

5 *Lenin's note*: Instead of 'Social-Democracy', whose
official leaders *throughout* the world have betrayed socialism
and deserted to the bourgeoisie (the 'defencists' and the
vacillating 'Kautskyites'), we must call ourselves the Communist Party.

6 *Lenin's note*: The 'Centre' in the international Social-
Democratic movement is the trend which vacillates
between the chauvinists (= 'defencists') and internationalists, i.e. Kautsky and Co. in Germany, Longuet and Co.
in France, Chkheidze and Co. in Russia, Turati and Co. in
Italy, MacDonald and Co. in Britain, etc.

planted the banner of civil war in the midst of revolutionary democracy' (quoted in No. 5 of Mr Plekhanov's *Yedinstvo*[7]).

Isn't it a gem?

I write, announce and elaborately explain: 'In view of the undoubted honesty of those *broad* sections of the *mass* believers in revolutionary defencism ... in view of the fact that they are being deceived by the bourgeoisie, it is necessary with particular thoroughness, persistence and patience to explain their error to them ...'

Yet the bourgeois gentlemen who call themselves Social-Democrats, who do not belong either to the *broad* sections or to the mass believers in defencism, with serene brow present my views thus: 'The banner [!][8] of civil war' (of which

---

7   *Yedinstvo* (Unity): a daily published in Petrograd from March to November 1917, and then under another name from December 1917 to January 1918. Edited by G. V. Plekhanov, it united the extreme right of the Menshevik defencists, gave unqualified support to the Provisional Government, and carried on a fierce struggle against the Bolshevik Party.

8   Interpolations in square brackets (within passages

there is not a word in the theses and not a word in my speech!) has been planted [!] 'in the midst [!!] of revolutionary democracy ...'

What does this mean? In what way does this differ from riot-inciting agitation, from *Russkaya Volya*?[9]

I write, announce and elaborately explain: 'The Soviets of Workers' Deputies are the *only possible* form of revolutionary government, and therefore our task is to present a patient, systematic, and persistent *explanation* of the errors of their tactics, an explanation especially adapted to the practical needs of the masses.'

Yet opponents of a certain brand present my views as a call to 'civil war in the midst of revolutionary democracy'!

I attacked the Provisional Government for *not*

---

quoted by Lenin) were introduced by Lenin himself. —*Ed.*

9   *Russkaya Volya* (Russian Freedom): a daily founded and run by the big banks. It appeared in Petrograd from December 1916 to October 1917 and carried on a riot-provoking campaign against the Bolsheviks.

having appointed an early date, or any date at all, for the convocation of the Constituent Assembly, and for confining itself to promises. I argued that *without* the Soviets of Workers' and Soldiers' Deputies the convocation of the Constituent Assembly is not guaranteed and its success is impossible.

And the view is attributed to me that I am opposed to the speedy convocation of the Constituent Assembly!

I would call this 'raving', had not decades of political struggle taught me to regard honesty in opponents as a rare exception.

Mr Plekhanov, in his paper, called my speech 'raving'. Very good, Mr Plekhanov! But look how awkward, uncouth, and slow-witted you are in your polemics. If I delivered a raving speech for two hours, how is it that an audience of hundreds tolerated this 'raving'? Further, why does your paper devote a whole column to an account of the 'raving'? Inconsistent, highly inconsistent!

It is, of course, much easier to shout, abuse, and howl than to attempt to relate, to explain, to recall *what* Marx and Engels said in 1871, 1872 and 1875 about the experience of the Paris Commune and about the kind of state the proletariat needs.

Ex-Marxist Mr Plekhanov evidently does not care to recall Marxism.

I quoted the words of Rosa Luxemburg, who on 4 August 1914, called *German* Social-Democracy a 'stinking corpse'. And the Plekhanovs, Goldenbergs and Co. feel 'offended'. On whose behalf? On behalf of the *German* chauvinists, because they were called chauvinists!

They have got themselves in a mess, these poor Russian social-chauvinists—socialists in word and chauvinists in deed.

Letters from Afar
(7–26 March 1917)[1]

V. I. Lenin

---

1 The first four 'Letters from Afar' were written between 7 and 12 (20 and 25) March; the fifth, unfinished letter was written on the eve of Lenin's departure from Switzerland, on 26 March (8 April) 1917. The first letter appeared in Nos 14 and 15 of *Pravda*, 21 and 22 March (3 and 4 April), with considerable abridgements and certain changes made by the editorial board, which included L. B. Kamenev and J.V. Stalin. The second, third and fourth letters were not published in 1917.

First Letter

The first stage of the first revolution[2]

The first revolution engendered by the imperialist world war has broken out. The first revolution but certainly not the last. Judging by the scanty information available in Switzerland, the first stage of this first revolution, namely, of the *Russian* revolution of 1 March 1917, has ended. This first stage of our revolution will certainly not be the last.

How could such a 'miracle' have happened, that in only eight days—the period indicated by Mr

---

2   The *Pravda* editors deleted about one fifth of the first letter. The cuts chiefly concerned Lenin's characterization of the Menshevik and Socialist-Revolutionary leaders as conciliators and flunkeys of the bourgeoisie, their attempts to hide from the people the fact that representatives of the British and French governments helped the Cadets and Octobrists secure the abdication of Nicholas II, and also Lenin's exposure of the monarchist and imperialist proclivities of the Provisional Government, which was determined to continue the predatory war.

Milyukov in his boastful telegram to all Russia's representatives abroad—a monarchy collapsed that had maintained itself for centuries, and that in spite of everything had managed to maintain itself throughout the three years of the tremendous, nation-wide class battles of 1905–1907?

There are no miracles in nature or history, but every abrupt turn in history, and this applies to every revolution, presents such a wealth of content, unfolds such unexpected and specific combinations of forms of struggle and alignment of forces of the contestants, that to the lay mind there is much that must appear miraculous.

The combination of a number of factors of world-historic importance was required for the tsarist monarchy to have collapsed in a few days. We shall mention the chief of them.

Without the tremendous class battles and the revolutionary energy displayed by the Russian proletariat during the three years 1905–1907, the second revolution could not possibly have been so rapid in the sense that its *initial stage* was completed in a few days. The first revolution (1905) deeply ploughed the soil, uprooted age-old prej-udices, awakened millions of workers and tens of millions of peasants to political life and political struggle and revealed to each other—and to the world—*all* classes (and all the principal parties) of Russian society in their true character and in the true alignment of their interests, their forces, their modes of action, and their immediate and ultimate aims. This first revolution, and the suc-ceeding period of counter-revolution (1907–14), laid bare the very essence of the tsarist mon-archy, brought it to the 'utmost limit', exposed all the rottenness and infamy, the cynicism and corruption of the tsar's clique, dominated by that monster, Rasputin. It exposed all the bes-tiality of the Romanov family—those pogrom-mongers who drenched Russia in the blood of Jews, workers and revolutionaries, those *landlords*, 'first among peers', *who own millions* of dessiatines of land and are prepared to stoop to any brutality, to any crime, to ruin and strangle any number of citizens in order to preserve the 'sacred right of property' for themselves *and their class*.

Without the Revolution of 1905–1907 and the counter-revolution of 1907–1914, there could not have been that clear 'self-determination' of all classes of the Russian people and of the nations inhabiting Russia, that determination of the relation of these classes to each other and to the tsarist monarchy, which manifested itself during the eight days of the February–March Revolution of 1917. This eight-day revolution was 'performed', if we may use a metaphorical expression, as though after a dozen major and minor rehearsals; the 'actors' knew each other, their parts, their places and their setting in every detail, through and through, down to every more or less important shade of political trend and mode of action.

For the first great Revolution of 1905, which the Guchkovs and Milyukovs and their hangers-on denounced as a 'great rebellion', led, after the lapse of twelve years, to the 'brilliant', the 'glorious' Revolution of 1917—the Guchkovs and Milyukovs have proclaimed it 'glorious' because it has put them in power (*for the time being*). But this required a great, mighty and all-powerful 'stage manager', capable, on the one hand, of vastly accelerating the course of world history, and, on the other, of engendering world-wide crises of unparalleled intensity—economic, political, national and international. Apart from an extraordinary acceleration of world history, it was also necessary that history make particularly abrupt turns, in order that at one such turn the filthy and blood-stained cart of the Romanov monarchy should be overturned *at one stroke*.

This all-powerful 'stage manager', this mighty accelerator, was the imperialist world war.

That it is a world war is now indisputable, for the United States and China are already half-involved today, and will be fully involved tomorrow.

That it is an imperialist war on *both* sides is now likewise indisputable. Only the capitalists and their hangers-on, the social-patriots and social-chauvinists, or—if instead of general critical definitions we use political names familiar in Russia—only the Guchkovs and Lvovs, Milyukovs and Shingaryovs on the one hand,

and only the Gvozdyovs, Potresovs, Chkhenkelis, Kerenskys and Chkheidzes on the other, can deny or gloss over this fact. *Both* the German and the Anglo-French bourgeoisie are waging the war for the plunder of foreign countries and the strangling of small nations, for financial world supremacy and the division and redivision of colonies, and in order to save the tottering capitalist regime by misleading and dividing the workers of the various countries.

The imperialist war was bound, with objective inevitability, immensely to accelerate and intensify to an unprecedented degree the class struggle of the proletariat against the bourgeoisie; it was bound to turn into a civil war between the hostile classes.

This *transformation has been started* by the February–March Revolution of 1917, the first stage of which has been marked, firstly, by a joint blow at tsarism struck by two forces: one, the whole of bourgeois and landlord Russia, with all her unconscious hangers-on and all her conscious leaders, the British and French ambassadors and capitalists, and the other, *the Soviet of Workers' Deputies*, which has begun to win over the soldiers' and peasants' deputies.[3]

These three political camps, these three fundamental political forces—(1) the tsarist monarchy, the head of the feudal landlords, of the old bureaucracy and the military caste; (2) bourgeois and landlord-Octobrist-Cadet Russia,[4] behind which trailed the petty bourgeoisie (of which Kerensky and Chkheidze are the principal representatives);

---

3 Lenin here refers to the Petrograd Soviet of Workers' Deputies, which emerged in the very early days of the February Revolution. Elections to the Soviet began spontaneously at individual factories and within a few days spread to all the factories in the capital.

4 Octobrists: members of the Union of October Seventeen, a counter-revolutionary party formed after promulgation of the tsar's Manifesto of 17 (30) October 1905. It represented and upheld the interests of the big bourgeoisie and of the landlords who ran their estates on capitalist lines. Cadets: the name derives from the Constitutional-Democratic Party, the chief party of the Russian liberal-monarchist bourgeoisie. Founded in October 1905, it was composed chiefly of capitalists, landlords and bourgeois intellectuals.

(3) the Soviet of Workers' Deputies, which is seeking to make the entire proletariat and the entire mass of the poorest part of the population its allies—these three *fundamental* political forces fully and clearly revealed themselves even in the eight days of the 'first stage' and even to an observer so remote from the scene of events as the present writer, who is obliged to content himself with the meagre foreign press dispatches.

But before dealing with this in greater detail, I must return to the part of my letter devoted to a factor of prime importance, namely, the imperialist world war.

The war shackled the belligerent powers, the belligerent groups of capitalists, the 'bosses' of the capitalist system, the slave-owners of the capitalist slave system, to each other with *chains of iron. One bloody clot*—such is the social and political life of the present moment in history.

The socialists who deserted to the bourgeoisie on the outbreak of the war—all these Davids and Scheidemanns in Germany and the Plekhanovs, Potresovs, Gvozdyovs and Co. in Russia—

clamoured loud and long against the 'illusions' of the revolutionaries, against the 'illusions' of the Basle Manifesto, against the 'farcical dream' of turning the imperialist war into a civil war. They sang praises in every key to the strength, tenacity and adaptability allegedly revealed by capitalism—*they*, who had aided the capitalists to 'adapt', tame, mislead and divide the working classes of the various countries!

But 'he who laughs last laughs best'. The bourgeoisie has been unable to delay for long the revolutionary crisis engendered by the war. That crisis is growing with irresistible force in all countries, beginning with Germany, which, according to an observer who recently visited that country, is suffering 'brilliantly organized famine', and ending with England and France, where *famine is also* looming, but where organization is far less 'brilliant'.

It was natural that the revolutionary crisis should have broken out *first of all* in tsarist Russia, where the disorganization was most appalling and the proletariat most revolutionary (not by virtue of any special qualities, but because of the living traditions of 1905). This crisis was precipitated by the series of extremely severe defeats sustained by Russia and her allies. They shook up the old machinery of government and the old order and roused the anger of *all* classes of the population against them; they embittered the army, wiped out a very large part of the old commanding personnel, composed of die-hard aristocrats and exceptionally corrupt bureaucratic elements, and replaced it by a young, fresh, mainly bourgeois, commoner, petty-bourgeois personnel. Those who, grovelling to the bourgeoisie or simply lacking backbone, howled and wailed about 'defeatism', are now faced by the fact of the historical connection between the defeat of the most backward and barbarous tsarist monarchy and the *beginning* of the revolutionary conflagration.

But while the defeats early in the war were a negative factor that precipitated the upheaval, the *connection* between Anglo-French finance capital, Anglo-French imperialism, and Russian

Octobrist-Cadet capital was a factor that hastened this crisis by the direct *organization of a plot*
against Nicholas Romanov.

This highly important aspect of the situation is, for obvious reasons, hushed up by the
Anglo-French press and maliciously emphasized
by the German. We Marxists must soberly face
the truth and not allow ourselves to be con-
fused either by the lies, the official sugary dip-
lomatic and ministerial lies, of the first group of
imperialist belligerents, or by the sniggering and
smirking of their financial and military rivals of
the other belligerent group. The whole course
of events in the February–March Revolution
clearly shows that the British and French embas-
sies, with their agents and 'connections', who
had long been making the most desperate efforts
to prevent 'separate' agreements and a separate
peace between Nicholas II (and last, we hope,
and we will endeavour to make him that) and
Wilhelm II, directly organized a plot in conjunc-
tion with the Octobrists and Cadets, in conjunc-
tion with a section of the generals and army and

St Petersburg garrison officers, with the express object of *deposing* Nicholas Romanov.

Let us not harbour any illusions. Let us not make the mistake of those who—like certain OC supporters or Mensheviks who are oscillating between Gvozdyov-Potresov policy and internationalism and only too often slip into petty-bourgeois pacifism—are now ready to extol 'agreement' between the workers' party and the Cadets, 'support' of the latter by the former, etc. In conformity with the old (and by no means Marxist) doctrine that they have learned by rote, they are trying to veil the plot of the Anglo-French imperialists and the Guchkovs and Milyukovs aimed at deposing the 'chief warrior', Nicholas Romanov, and putting more energetic, fresh and more capable *warriors* in his place.

That the revolution succeeded so quickly and—seemingly, at the first superficial glance— so radically, is only due to the fact that, as a result of an extremely unique historical situation, *absolutely dissimilar currents*, *absolutely heterogeneous* class interests, *absolutely contrary* political and social strivings have merged, and in a strikingly 'harmonious' manner. Namely, the conspiracy of the Anglo-French imperialists, who impelled Milyukov, Guchkov and Co. to seize power *for the purpose of continuing the imperialist war*, for the purpose of conducting the war still more ferociously and obstinately, for the purpose of *slaughtering fresh millions* of Russian workers and peasants in order that the Guchkovs might obtain Constantinople, the French capitalists Syria, the British capitalists Mesopotamia, and so on. This on the one hand. On the other, there was a profound proletarian and mass popular movement of a revolutionary character (a movement of the entire poorest section of the population of town and country) for *bread*, for *peace*, for *real freedom*.

It would simply be foolish to speak of the revolutionary proletariat of Russia 'supporting' the Cadet-Octobrist imperialism, which has been 'patched up' with English money and is as abominable as tsarist imperialism. The revolutionary workers were destroying, have already destroyed to a considerable degree and will destroy to its foundations the infamous tsarist *monarchy*. They are neither elated nor dismayed by the fact that at certain brief and exceptional historical conjunctures *they were aided* by the struggle of Buchanan, Guchkov, Milyukov and Co. to *replace* one monarch by *another monarch*, also preferably a Romanov!

Such, and only such, is the way the situation developed. Such, and only such, in the view that can be taken by a politician who does not fear the truth, who soberly weighs the balance of social forces in the revolution, who appraises every 'current situation' not only from the standpoint of all its present, current peculiarities, but also from the standpoint of the more fundamental motivations, the deeper interest-relationship of the proletariat and the bourgeoisie, both in Russia and throughout the world.

The workers of Petrograd, like the workers of the whole of Russia, self-sacrificingly fought the tsarist monarchy—fought for freedom, land for the peasants, and *for peace*, against the imperialist slaughter. To continue and intensify that slaughter,

Anglo-French imperialist capital hatched Court intrigues, conspired with the officers of the Guards, incited and encouraged the Guchkovs and Milyukov, and fixed up a *complete new government*, which in fact *did seize power* immediately the proletarian struggle had struck the first blows at tsarism.

This new government, in which Lvov and Guchkov of the Octobrists and Peaceful Renovation Party,[5] yesterday's abettors of Stolypin the Hangman, control *really important* posts, vital posts, decisive posts, the army and the bureaucracy —this government, in which Milyukov and the other Cadets are more than anything decorations, a signboard—they are there to deliver sentimental professorial speeches—and in which the Trudovik[6] Kerensky is a balalaika on which

---

5 Peaceful Renovation Party: a constitutional-monarchist organization of the big bourgeoisie and land-lords that took final shape in 1906 following the dissolution of the First Duma.

6 Trudovik: member of the Trudovik group in the State Dumas formed in April 1906 by petty-bourgeois democrats. The group wavered between the Cadets and the

they play to deceive the workers and peasants—
this government is not a fortuitous assemblage of
persons.

They are representatives of the new class that
has risen to political power in Russia, the class
of capitalist landlords and bourgeoisie which has
long been *ruling* our country economically, and
which during the Revolution of 1905–1907,
the counter-revolutionary period of 1907–1914,
and finally—and with especial rapidity—the war
period of 1914–1917, was quick to organize itself
politically, taking over control of the local government bodies, public education, congresses of
various types, the Duma, the war industries committees, etc. This new class was already 'almost
completely' *in* power by 1917, and therefore it
needed only the first blows to bring tsarism to
the ground and clear the way for the bourgeoisie.
The imperialist war, which required an incredi-
ble exertion of effort, so accelerated the course of

revolutionary Social-Democrats. After the October Revolution the Trudoviks sided with the counter-revolutionary
forces.

backward Russia's development that we have 'at one blow' (*seemingly* at one blow) *caught up* with Italy, England, and almost with France. We have obtained a 'coalition', a 'national' (i.e., adapted for carrying on the imperialist slaughter and for fooling the people) 'parliamentary' government.

Side by side with this government—which as regards the *present* war is but the agent of the billion-dollar 'firm' 'England and France'—there has arisen the chief, unofficial, as yet undeveloped and comparatively weak *workers' government*, which expresses the interests of the proletariat and of the entire poor section of the urban and rural population. This is the *Soviet of Workers' Deputies* in Petrograd, which is seeking connections with the soldiers and peasants, and also with the agricultural workers—with the latter particularly and primarily, of course, more than with the peasants.

Such is the *actual* political situation, which we must first endeavour to define with the greatest possible objective precision, in order that Marxist tactics may be based upon the only possible solid foundation—the foundation of *facts*.

The tsarist monarchy has been smashed, but not finally destroyed.

The Octobrist-Cadet bourgeois government, which wants to fight the imperialist war 'to a finish', and which in reality is the agent of the financial arm 'England and France', is *obliged to promise* the people the maximum of liberties and sops compatible with the maintenance of its power over the people and the possibility of continuing the imperialist slaughter.

The Soviet of Workers' Deputies is an organization of the workers, the embryo of a workers' government, the representative of the interests of the entire mass of the *poor* section of the population, i.e., of nine-tenths of the population, which is striving for *peace*, *bread* and *freedom*.

The conflict of these three forces determines the situation that has now arisen, a situation that is *transitional* from the first stage of the revolution to the second.

The antagonism between the first and second force is *not* profound, it is temporary, the result *solely* of the present conjuncture of circumstances, of the abrupt turn of events in the imperialist war. The *whole* of the new government is monarchist, for Kerensky's *verbal* republicanism simply cannot be taken seriously, is not worthy of a statesman and, *objectively*, is political chicanery. The new government, which has not dealt the tsarist monarchy the final blow, has already *begun to strike a bargain* with the landlord Romanov dynasty. The bourgeoisie of the Octobrist-Cadet type *needs* a monarchy to serve as the head of the bureaucracy and the army in order to protect the privileges of capital against the working people.

He who says that the workers must support the new government in the interests of the struggle against tsarist reaction (and apparently this is being said by the Potresovs, Gvozdyovs, Chkhenkelis and also, all *evasiveness* notwithstanding, by *Chkheidze*) is a traitor to the workers, a traitor to the cause of the proletariat, to the cause of peace and freedom. For actually, *precisely* this new government is *already* bound hand and foot by imperialist capital, by the imperialist policy of *war* and plunder, has *already* begun to strike a bargain (without consulting the people!) with the dynasty, *is already working to restore the tsarist monarchy*, is already soliciting the candidature of Mikhail Romanov as the new kinglet, is already taking measures to prop up the throne, to substitute for the legitimate (lawful, ruling by virtue of the old law) monarchy a Bonapartist, plebiscite monarchy (ruling by virtue of a fraudulent plebiscite).

No, if there is to be a real struggle against the tsarist monarchy, if freedom is to be guaranteed in fact and not merely in words, in the glib promises of Milyukov and Kerensky, the workers must not support the new government; the government must 'support' the workers! For the only guarantee of freedom and of the complete destruction of tsarism lies in *arming the proletariat*, in strengthening, extending and developing the role, significance and power of the Soviet of Workers' Deputies.

All the rest is mere phrase-mongering and lies, self-deception on the part of the politicians of the liberal and radical camp, fraudulent trickery.

Help, or at least do not hinder, the arming of the workers, and freedom in Russia will be invincible, the monarchy irrestorable, the republic secure.

Otherwise the Guchkovs and Milyukovs will restore the monarchy and grant *none*, absolutely none of the 'liberties' they promised. All bourgeois politicians in *all* bourgeois revolutions 'fed' the people and fooled the workers with promises.

Ours is a bourgeois revolution, *therefore*, the workers must support the bourgeoisie, say the Potresovs, Gvozdyovs and Chkheidzes, as Plekhanov said yesterday.

Ours is a bourgeois revolution, we Marxists say, *therefore* the workers must open the eyes of the people to the deception practised by the bourgeois politicians, teach them to put no faith in words, to depend entirely on their *own* strength, their *own* organization, their *own* unity, and their *own weapons*.

The government of the Octobrists and Cadets, of the Guchkovs and Milyukovs, *cannot*, even if it sincerely wanted to (only infants can think that Guchkov and Lvov are sincere), *cannot* give the people either *peace*, *bread*, or *freedom*.

It cannot give peace because it is a war government, a government for the continuation of the imperialist slaughter, a government of *plunder*, out to plunder Armenia, Galicia and Turkey, annex Constantinople, reconquer Poland, Courland, Lithuania, etc. It is a government bound hand and foot by Anglo-French imperialist capital. Russian capital is merely a branch of the world-wide 'firm' which manipulates *hundreds of billions* of roubles and is called 'England and France'.

It cannot give bread because it is a bourgeois government. *At best*, it can give the people 'brilliantly organized famine', as Germany has done. But the people will not accept famine. They will learn, and probably very soon, that there is bread and that it can be obtained, but only by methods that *do not respect the sanctity of capital and land ownership*.

It cannot give freedom because it is a landlord and capitalist government which fears the people and has already begun to strike a bargain with the Romanov dynasty.

The tactical problems of our immediate attitude towards this government will be dealt with in another article. In it, we shall explain the peculiarity of the present situation, which is a *transition* from the first stage of the revolution to the second, and why the slogan, the 'task of the day', at *this* moment must be: *Workers, you have performed miracles of proletarian heroism, the heroism of the people, in the civil war against tsarism. You must perform miracles of organization, organization of the proletariat and of the whole people, to prepare the way for your victory in the second stage of the revolution.*

Confining ourselves for the *present* to an analysis of the class struggle and the alignment of class forces at this stage of the revolution, we have still to put the question: who are the proletariat's *allies* in *this* revolution?

It has *two* allies: first, the broad mass of the semi-proletarian and partly also of the small-peasant population, who number scores of millions and constitute the overwhelming majority of the population of Russia. For this mass, peace, bread, freedom and land are *essential*. It is inevitable that to a certain extent this mass will be under the influence of the bourgeoisie, particularly of the petty bourgeoisie, to which it is most akin in its conditions of life, vacillating between the bourgeoisie and the proletariat. The cruel lessons of war, and they will be the *more* cruel the more vigorously the war is prosecuted by Guchkov, Lvov, Milyukov and Co., will *inevitably* push this mass towards the proletariat, compel it to follow the proletariat. We must now take advantage of the relative freedom of the new order and of the Soviets of Workers' Deputies to *enlighten* and *organize* this mass first of all and above all. Soviets of Peasants' Deputies and Soviets of Agricultural Workers—that is one of our most urgent tasks. In this connection we shall strive not only for the agricultural workers to establish their own separate Soviets, but also for the propertyless and poorest peasants to organize *separately* from the well-to-do peasants. The special tasks and special forms of organization urgently needed at the present time will be dealt with in the next letter.

Second, the ally of the Russian proletariat is the proletariat of all the belligerent countries and of all countries in general. At present this ally is to a large degree repressed by the war, and all too often the European social-chauvinists speak in its name—men who, like Plekhanov, Gvozdyov and Potresov in Russia, have deserted to the bourgeoisie. But the liberation of the proletariat from their influence has progressed with every month of the imperialist war, and the Russian revolution will *inevitably* immensely hasten this process.

With these two allies, the proletariat, *utilizing the peculiarities* of the present transition situation, can and will proceed, first, to the achievement of a democratic republic and complete victory of the peasantry over the landlords, instead of the Guchkov-Milyukov semi-monarchy, and then to *socialism*, which alone can give the war-weary people *peace*, *bread* and *freedom*.

Second Letter

The new government and the proletariat

The principal document I have at my disposal at today's date, 8 (21) March, is a copy of that most conservative and bourgeois English newspaper *The Times* of 16 March, containing a batch of reports about the revolution in Russia. Clearly, a source more favourably inclined—to put it mildly—towards the Guchkov and Milyukov government it would not be easy to find.

This newspaper's correspondent reports from St Petersburg on Wednesday, 1 (14) March, when the *first* Provisional government still existed, i.e., the thirteen-member Duma Executive Committee,[7] headed by Rodzyanko and includ-

---

7   The first Provisional Government, or the Provisional Committee of the State Duma, was formed on 27 February (12 March) 1917. On that day the Duma Council of Doyens sent a telegram to the tsar drawing his attention to the critical situation in the capital and urging immediate

ing two 'socialists', as the newspaper puts it, Kerensky and Chkheidze:

'A group of 22 elected members of the Upper House [State Council] including M. Guchkov, M. Stakhovich, Prince Trubetskoi, and Professor Vassiliev, Grimm, and Vernadsky, yesterday addressed a telegram to the Tsar' imploring him in order to save the 'dynasty', etc., etc., to convoke the Duma and to name as the head of the government someone who enjoys the 'confidence of the nation'. 'What the Emperor may decide to do on his arrival today is unknown at the hour of telegraphing', writes the correspondent, 'but one thing is quite certain. Unless His

---

measures 'to save the fatherland and the dynasty'. The tsar replied by sending the Duma President, M.V. Rodzyanko, a decree dissolving the Duma. By this time the insurgent people had surrounded the Duma building, the Tauride Palace, where Duma members were meeting in private conference, and blocked all the streets leading to it. Soldiers and armed workers were in occupation of the building. In this situation the Duma hastened to elect a Provisional Committee to 'maintain order in Petrograd and for communication with various institutions and individuals'.

Majesty immediately complies with the wishes of the most moderate elements among his loyal subjects, the influence at present exercised by the Provisional Committee of the Imperial Duma will pass wholesale into the hands of the social- ists, who want to see a republic established, but who are unable to institute any kind of orderly government and would inevitably precipitate the country into anarchy within and disaster without ...'

What political sagacity and clarity this reveals. How well this Englishman, who thinks like (if he does not guide) the Guchkovs and Milyukovs, understands the alignment of class forces and interests! 'The most moderate elements among his loyal subjects', i.e., the monarchist landlords and capitalists, want to take power into their hands, fully realizing that otherwise 'influence' will pass into the hands of the 'socialists'. Why the 'socialists' and not somebody else? Because the English Guchkovite is fully aware that there is *no* other social force in the political arena, *nor can there be*. The revolution was made by the proletariat. It displayed heroism; it shed its blood; it swept along with it the broadest masses of the toilers and the poor; it is demanding bread, peace and freedom; it is demanding a republic; it sympathizes with socialism. But the handful of landlords and capitalists headed by the Guchkovs and Milyukovs want to betray the will, or strivings, of the vast majority and conclude *a deal with the loitering monarchy*, bolster it up, save it: appoint Lvov and Guchkov, Your Majesty, and we will be with the monarchy against the people. Such is the entire meaning, the sum and substance of the new government's policy!

But how to justify the deception, the fooling of the people, the violation of the will of the overwhelming majority of the population?

By slandering the people—the old but eternally new method of the bourgeoisie. And the English Guchkovite slanders, scolds, spits and splutters: 'anarchy within and disaster without', no 'orderly government'!!

That is not true, Mr Guchkovite! The workers want a republic; and a republic represents far more 'orderly' government than monarchy does. What guarantee have the people that the second Romanov will not get himself a second Rasputin? Disaster will be brought on precisely by continuation of the war, i.e., precisely by the new government. Only a proletarian republic, backed by the rural workers and the poorest section of the peasants and town dwellers, can secure peace, provide bread, order and freedom.

All the shouts about anarchy are merely a screen to conceal the selfish interests of the capitalists, who want to make profit out of the war, out of war loans, who want to restore the monarchy *against* the people.

'Yesterday', continues the correspondent, 'the Social-Democratic Party issued a proclamation of a most seditious character, which was spread broadcast throughout the city. They [i.e., the Social-Democratic Party] are mere doctrinaires, but their power for mischief is enormous at a time like the present. M. Kerensky and M. Chkheidze, who realize that without the support of the officers and the more moderate elements of the people they cannot hope to avoid anarchy, have to reckon with their less prudent associates, and are insensibly driven to take up an attitude which complicates the task of the Provisional Committee...'

O great English, Guchkovite diplomat! How 'imprudently' you have blurted out the truth!

'The Social-Democratic Party' and 'their less prudent associates', with whom Kerensky and Chkheidze 'have to reckon', evidently mean the Central or the St Petersburg Committee of our Party, which was restored at the January 1912 Conference, those very same Bolsheviks at whom the bourgeoisie always hurl the abusive term 'doctrinaires', because of their faithfulness to the 'doctrine', i.e., the fundamentals, the principles, teachings, aims of *socialism*. Obviously, the English Guchkovite hurls the abusive terms seditious and doctrinaire at the manifesto[8] and

---

8 This refers to the *Manifesto of the Russian Social-Democratic Labour Party to All Citizens of Russia*, issued by the Central Committee and published as a supplement to *Izvestia* of 28 February (13 March) 1917 (No. 1). Lenin

at the conduct of our Party in urging a fight for
a republic, peace, complete destruction of the
tsarist monarchy, bread for the people.

Bread for the people and peace—that's sedi-
tion, but ministerial posts for Guchkov and
Milyukov—that's 'order'. Old and familiar talk!

What, then, are the tactics of Kerensky and
Chkheidze as characterized by the English
Guchkovite?

Vacillation: on the one hand, the Guchkovite
praises them: they 'realize' (Good boys! Clever
boys!) that without the 'support' of the army officers and the more moderate elements, anarchy
cannot be avoided (we, however, have always
thought, in keeping with our doctrine, with our
socialist teachings, that it is the capitalists who
introduce anarchy and war into human society,

---

learned of the Manifesto from an abridged version in the
morning edition of the *Frankfurter Zeitung*, 9 (22) March
1917. On the following day he wired *Pravda* in Petrograd
via Oslo: 'Have just read excerpts from the Central Committee Manifesto. Best wishes. Long live the proletarian
militia, harbinger of peace and socialism!'

that only the transfer of *all* political power to the proletariat and the poorest people can rid us of war, of anarchy and starvation!). On the other hand, they 'have to reckon with their less prudent associates', i.e., the Bolsheviks, the Russian Social-Democratic Labour Party, restored and united by the Central Committee.

What is the force that compels Kerensky and Chkheidze to 'reckon' with the Bolshevik Party to which they have never belonged, which they, or their literary representatives (Socialist-Revolutionaries, Popular Socialists, the Menshevik OC supporters, and so forth), have always abused, condemned, denounced as an insignificant underground circle, a sect of doctrinaires, and so forth? Where and when has it ever happened that in time of revolution, at a time of predominantly *mass* action, sane-minded politicians should 'reckon' with 'doctrinaires'??

He is all mixed up, our poor English Guchkovite; he has failed to produce a logical argument, has failed to tell either a whole lie or the whole truth, he has merely given himself away.

Kerensky and Chkheidze are compelled to reckon with the Social-Democratic Party of the Central Committee by the influence it exerts on the proletariat, on the masses. Our Party was found to be with the masses, with the revolutionary proletariat, *in spite of* the arrest and deportation of our Duma deputies to Siberia, as far back as 1914; in spite of the fierce persecution and arrests to which the St Petersburg Committee was subjected for its underground activities during the war, *against* the war and against tsarism.

'Facts are stubborn things', as the English proverb has it. Let me remind you of it, most esteemed English Guchkovite! That our Party guided, or at least rendered devoted assistance to, the St Petersburg workers in the great days of revolution is a fact the English Guchkovite '*himself*' was *obliged* to admit. And he was equally obliged to admit the fact that Kerensky and Chkheidze are oscillating *between* the bourgeoisie and the proletariat. The Gvozdyovites, the 'defencists', i.e., the social-chauvinists, i.e., the defenders of the imperialist, predatory war, are now completely following the bourgeoisie; Kerensky, by entering the ministry, i.e., the second Provisional Government, has also completely deserted to the bourgeoisie; Chkheidze has not; he continues to *oscillate* between the Provisional Government of the bourgeoisie, the Guchkovs and Milyukovs, and the 'provisional government' of the proletariat and the poorest masses of the people, the Soviet of Workers' Deputies and the Russian Social-Democratic Labour Party united by the Central Committee.

Consequently, the revolution has confirmed what we especially insisted on when we urged the workers clearly to realize the class difference between the principal parties and principal trends in the working-class movement and among the petty bourgeoisie—what we wrote, for example, in the Geneva *Sotsial-Demokrat* No. 41, nearly eighteen months ago, on 13 October 1915:

As hitherto, we consider it admissible for Social-Democrats to join a provisional revolutionary government together with the democratic petty bourgeoisie, but *not* with the revolutionary chauvinists. By revolutionary chauvinists we mean those who want a victory over tsarism so as to achieve victory over Germany—plunder other countries—consolidate Great-Russian rule over the other peoples of Russia, etc. Revolutionary chauvinism is based on the class position of the petty bourgeoisie. The latter always vacillates between the bourgeoisie and the proletariat. At present it is vacillating between chauvinism (which prevents it from being consistently revolutionary, even in the meaning of a democratic revolution) and proletarian internationalism. At the moment the Trudoviks, the Socialist-Revolutionaries, *Nasha Zarya* (now *Dyelo*), Chkheidze's Duma group, the Organizing Committee, Mr Plekhanov and the like are political spokesmen for this petty bourgeoisie in Russia. If the revolutionary chauvinists won in Russia, we would be opposed to a defence of *their* 'fatherland' in the present war. Our slogan is: against the chauvinists, even if they are revolutionary and republican—*against* them and *for* an alliance of the international proletariat for the socialist revolution.

But let us return to the English Guchkovite.

'The Provisional Committee of the Imperial Duma', he continues, 'appreciating the dangers ahead, have purposely refrained from carrying out the original intention of arresting Ministers, although they could have done so yesterday without the slightest difficulty. The door is thus left open for negotiations, thanks to which we ['we' = British finance capital and imperialism] may obtain all the benefits of the new regime without passing through the dread ordeal of the Commune and the anarchy of civil war ...'

The Guchkovites were *for* a civil war from which *they* would benefit, but they are *against* a civil war from which the people, i.e., the actual majority of the working people, would benefit.

The relations between the Provisional Committee of the Duma, which represents the whole nation [imagine saying this about the committee of the landlord and capitalist Fourth Duma!], and the Council of Labour Deputies, representing purely class interests [this is the language of a diplo-mat who has heard learned words with one ear and wants to conceal the fact that the Soviet of Workers' Deputies represents the proletariat and the poor, i.e., nine-tenths of the population], but in a crisis like the present wielding enormous power, have aroused no small misgivings among reasonable men regarding the possibility of a con-flict between them—the results of which might be too terrible to describe.

Happily this danger has been averted, at least for the present [note the 'at least'!], thanks to the influence of M. Kerensky, a young lawyer of much oratorical ability, who clearly realizes [unlike Chkheidze, who also 'realized', but evidently less clearly in the opinion of the Guchkovite?] the necessity of working with the Committee in the interests of his Labour constituents [i.e., to catch the workers' votes, to flirt with them]. A satisfac-tory Agreement[9] was concluded today [Wednesday,

9 The reference is to the agreement concluded on the night following 1 (14) March 1917 between the Duma Provisional Committee and the Socialist-Revolutionary

1 (14) March], whereby all unnecessary friction will be avoided.

What this agreement was, whether it was concluded with the *whole* of the Soviet of Workers' Deputies and on what terms, we do not know. On this *chief* point, the English Guchkovite says nothing at all this time. And no wonder! It is not to the advantage of the bourgeoisie to have these terms made clear, precise and known to all, for it would then be more difficult for it to violate them!

The preceding lines were already written when I read two very important communications. First, in that most conservative and bourgeois Paris newspaper *Le Temps*[10] of 20 March, the text

and Menshevik leaders of the Petrograd Soviet Executive Committee. The latter voluntarily surrendered power to the bourgeoisie, and authorized the Duma Provisional Committee to form a Provisional Government of its own choice.

10 *Le Temps*: a daily paper published in Paris from 1861 to 1942. It spoke for the ruling element, and was the factual organ of the French Foreign Ministry.

of the Soviet of Workers' Deputies manifesto appealing for 'support' of the new government;[11] second, excerpts from Skobelev's speech in the State Duma on 1 (14) March, reproduced in a Zurich newspaper (*Neue Zürcher Zeitung*, 1 Mit.-bl., 21 March) from a Berlin newspaper (*National-Zeitung*).

The manifesto of the Soviet of Workers' Deputies, if the text has not been distorted by the French imperialists, is a most remarkable document. It shows that the St Petersburg proletariat, at least at the time the manifesto was issued, was under the predominating influence of petty-bourgeois politicians. You will recall that in

---

11   The *Manifesto of the Executive Committee of the Soviet of Workers' and Soldiers' Deputies* was published in *Izvestia* on 3 (16) March 1917 (No. 4), simultaneously with the announcement of the formation of a Provisional Government under Prince Lvov. Drawn up by the Socialist-Revolutionary and Menshevik members of the Executive Committee, it declared that the democratic forces would support the new government 'to the extent that it carries out its undertakings and wages a determined struggle against the old regime'.

this category of politicians I include, as has been already mentioned above, people of the type of Kerensky and Chkheidze.

In the manifesto we find two political ideas, and two slogans corresponding to them:

Firstly. The manifesto says that the government (the new one) consists of 'moderate elements'. A strange description, by no means complete, of a purely liberal, not of a Marxist character. I too am prepared to agree that in a certain sense— in my next letter I will show in precisely what sense—now, with the first stage of the revolution completed, every government must be 'moderate'. But it is absolutely impermissible to conceal from ourselves and from the people that this government wants to continue the imperialist war, that it is an agent of British capital, that it wants to restore the monarchy and strengthen the rule of the landlords and capitalists.

The manifesto declares that all democrats must 'support' the new government, and that the Soviet of Workers' Deputies requests and authorizes Kerensky to enter the Provisional Government.

The conditions—implementation of the promised reforms already during the war, guarantees for the 'free cultural' (only??) development of the nationalities (a purely Cadet, wretchedly liberal programme), and the establishment of a special committee consisting of members of the Soviet of Workers' Deputies and of 'military men'[12] to supervise the activities of the Provisional Government.

This Supervising Committee, which comes within the second category of ideas and slogans, we will discuss separately further on.

The appointment of the Russian Louis Blanc, Kerensky, and the appeal to support the new

---

12 The foreign press reported the appointment by the Petrograd Soviet of a special body to keep a check on the Provisional Government. On the basis of this report, Lenin at first welcomed the organization of this control body, pointing out, however, that only experience would show whether it would live up to expectations. Actually, this so-called Contact Committee, appointed by the Executive on 8 (21) March to 'influence' and 'control' the work of the Provisional Government, only helped the latter exploit the prestige of the Soviet as a cover for its counter-revolutionary policy.

government is, one may say, a classical example of betrayal of the cause of the revolution and the cause of the proletariat, a betrayal which doomed a number of nineteenth-century revolutions, irrespective of how sincere and devoted to socialism the leaders and supporters of such a policy may have been.

The proletariat cannot and must not support a war government, a restoration government. To fight reaction, to rebuff all possible and probable attempts by the Romanovs and their friends to restore the monarchy and muster a counter-revolutionary army, it is necessary not to support Guchkov and Co., but to *organize*, expand and strengthen a *proletarian* militia, to arm the people under the leadership of the workers. Without this principal, fundamental, radical measure, there can be no question either of offering serious resistance to the restoration of the monarchy and attempts to rescind or curtail the promised freedoms, or of firmly taking the road that will give the people bread, *peace* and freedom.

If it is true that Chkheidze, who, with Kerensky, was a member of the first Provisional Government (the Duma committee of thirteen), refrained from entering the second Provisional Government out of principled considerations of the above-mentioned or similar character, then that does him credit. That must be said frankly. Unfortunately, such an interpretation is contradicted by the facts, and primarily by the speech delivered by Skobelev, who has always gone hand in hand with Chkheidze.

Skobelev said, if the above-mentioned source is to be trusted, that 'the social [? evidently the Social-Democratic] group and the workers are only slightly in touch (have little contact) with the aims of the Provisional Government', that the workers are demanding peace, and that if the war is continued there will be disaster in the spring anyhow, that 'the workers have concluded with society [liberal society] a temporary agreement [*eine vorläufige Waffenfreundschaft*], although their political aims are as far removed from the aims of society as heaven is from earth', that 'the liberals must abandon the senseless [*unsinnige*] aims of the war', etc.

This speech is a sample of what we called above, in the excerpt from *Sotsial-Demokrat*, 'oscillation' between the bourgeoisie and the proletariat. The liberals, while remaining liberals, *cannot* 'abandon' the 'senseless' aims of the war, which, incidentally, are not determined by them alone, but by Anglo-French finance capital, a world-mighty force measured by hundreds of billions. The task is not to 'coax' the liberals, but to *explain* to the workers why the liberals find themselves in a blind alley, why *they* are bound hand and foot, why they *conceal* both the treaties tsarism concluded with England and other countries and the deals between Russian and Anglo-French capital, and so forth.

If Skobelev says that the workers have concluded an agreement with liberal society, no matter of what character, and since he does not protest against it, does not explain from the Duma rostrum how harmful it is for the workers, he thereby *approves* of the agreement. And that is exactly what he should not do.

Skobelev's direct or indirect, clearly expressed or tacit, approval of the agreement between the Soviet of Workers' Deputies and the Provisional Government is Skobelev's swing towards the bourgeoisie. Skobelev's statement that the workers are demanding peace, that their aims are as far removed from the liberals' aims as heaven is from earth, is Skobelev's swing towards the proletariat.

Purely proletarian, truly revolutionary and profoundly correct in design is the second political idea in the manifesto of the Soviet of Workers' Deputies that we are studying, namely, the idea of establishing a 'Supervising Committee' (I do not know whether this is what it is called in Russian; I am translating freely from the French), of proletarian-soldier supervision over the Provisional Government.

Now, that's something real! It is worthy of the workers who have shed their blood for freedom, peace, bread for the people! It is a *real step* towards *real guarantees* against tsarism, against a monarchy and against the monarchists Guchkov, Lvov and Co.! It is a sign that the Russian proletariat, in spite of everything, has made progress compared with the French proletariat in 1848, when it 'authorized' Louis Blanc! It is proof that the instinct and mind of the proletarian masses are not satisfied with declamations, exclamations, promises of reforms and freedoms, with the title of 'minister authorized by the workers', and similar tinsel, but are seeking support *only* where it is to be found, in the *armed* masses of the people organized and led by the proletariat, the class-conscious workers.

It is a step along the right road, but *only* the first step.

If this 'Supervising Committee' remains a purely political-type parliamentary institution, a committee that will 'put questions' to the Provisional Government and receive answers from it, then it will remain a plaything, will amount to nothing.

If, on the other hand, it leads, immediately and despite all obstacles, to the formation of a *workers' militia*, or *workers' home guard*, extending to the whole people, to all men and women, which would not only replace the exterminated and dissolved police force, not only make the latter's restoration *impossible* by *any* government, constitutional-monarchist or democratic-republican, *either* in St Petersburg *or* anywhere else in Russia—then the advanced workers of Russia will really take the road towards new and great victories, the road to victory over war, to the realization of the slogan which, as the newspapers report, adorned the colours of the cavalry troops that demonstrated in St Petersburg, in the square outside the State Duma:

'Long Live Socialist Republics in All Countries!'

I will set out my ideas about this workers' militia in my next letter.

In it I will try to show, on the one hand, that the formation of a militia embracing the entire people and led by the workers is the correct slogan of the day, one that corresponds to the tactical tasks of the peculiar transitional moment through which the Russian revolution (and the world revolution) is passing; and, on the other hand, that to be successful, this workers' militia must, firstly, embrace the entire people, must be a mass organization to the degree of being *universal*, must really embrace the *entire* able-bodied population of both sexes; secondly, it must proceed to combine not only purely police, but general state functions with military functions and with the control of social production and distribution.

N. Lenin

Zurich, 9 (22) March 1917

PS I forgot to date my previous letter 7 (20) March.

Third Letter

Concerning a proletarian militia

The conclusion I drew yesterday about Chkheidze's vacillating tactics has been fully confirmed today, 10 (23) March, by two documents. First—a telegraphic report from

Stockholm in the *Frankfurter Zeitung* containing excerpts from the manifesto of the Central Committee of our Party, the Russian Social-Democratic Labour Party, in St Petersburg. In this document there is not a word about either supporting the Guchkov government or overthrowing it; the workers and soldiers are called upon to organize around the Soviet of Workers' Deputies, to elect representatives to it for the fight against tsarism and for a republic, for an eight-hour day, for the confiscation of the landed estates and grain stocks, and chiefly, for an end to the predatory war. Particularly important and particularly urgent in this connection is our Central Committee's absolutely correct idea that to obtain peace, relations must be established with *the proletarians of all the belligerent countries*.

To expect peace from negotiations and relations between the bourgeois governments would be self-deception and deception of the people.

The second document is a Stockholm report, also by telegraph, to another German newspaper (*Vossische Zeitung*) about a conference between the Chkheidze group in the Duma, the workers' group (*Arbeiterfraktion*) and representatives of fifteen workers' unions on 2 (15) March and a manifesto published the next day. Of the eleven points of this manifesto, the telegram reports only three; the first, the demand for a republic; the seventh, the demand for peace and immediate peace negotiations; and the third, the demand for 'adequate participation in the government of representatives of the Russian working class'.

If this point is correctly reported, I can understand why the bourgeoisie is praising Chkheidze. I can understand why the praise of the English Guchkovites in *The Times* which I quoted elsewhere has been supplemented by the praise of the French Guchkovites in *Le Temps*. This newspaper of the French millionaires and imperialists writes on 22 March: 'The leaders of the workers' parties, particularly M. Chkheidze, are exercising all their influence to moderate the wishes of the working classes.'

Indeed, to demand workers' 'participation' in the Guchkov-Milyukov government is a theoretical and political absurdity: to participate as a minority would mean serving as a pawn; to participate on an 'equal footing' is impossible, because the demand to continue the war cannot be reconciled with the demand to conclude an armistice and start peace negotiations; to 'participate' as a majority requires the strength to *overthrow* the Guchkov-Milyukov government. In practice, the demand for 'participation' is the worst sort of Louis Blanc–ism, i.e., oblivion to the class struggle and the actual conditions under which it is being waged, infatuation with a most hollow-sounding phrase, spreading illusions among the workers, loss, in negotiations with Milyukov or Kerensky, of *precious* time which must be used to create a *real* class and revolutionary force, a proletarian militia that will *enjoy the confidence of all* the poor strata of the population, and they constitute the vast majority, and will *help them to organize*, help *them* to fight for bread, peace, freedom.

This mistake in the manifesto issued by Chkheidze and his group (I am not speaking of the OC, Organizing Committee *party*, because in the sources available to me there is not a word about the OC)—this mistake is all the more strange considering that at the 2 (15) March conference, Chkheidze's closest collaborator, Skobelev, said, according to the newspapers: 'Russia is on the eve of a second, real [*wirklich*] revolution.'

Now that is the truth, from which Skobelev and Chkheidze have forgotten to draw the practical conclusions. I cannot judge from here, from my accursed afar, how near this second revolution is. Being on the spot, Skobelev can see things better. Therefore, I am not raising for myself problems for the solution of which I have not and cannot have the necessary concrete data. I am merely emphasizing the confirmation by Skobelev, an 'outside witness', i.e., one who does not belong to our Party, of the *factual* conclusion I drew in my first letter, namely: that the February–March Revolution was merely the *first stage* of the revolution. Russia is passing through a peculiar historical moment of *transition* to the next stage of the revolution, or, to use Skobelev's expression, to a 'second revolution'.

If we want to be Marxists and learn from the experience of revolution in the whole world, we must strive to understand in what, precisely, lies the *peculiarity* of this *transitional* moment, and what tactics follow from its objective specific features.

The peculiarity of the situation lies in that the Guchkov-Milyukov government gained the first victory with extraordinary ease due to the following three major circumstances: (1) assistance from Anglo-French finance capital and its agents; (2) assistance from part of the top ranks of the army; (3) the already existing organization of the entire Russian bourgeoisie in the shape of the rural and urban local government institutions, the State Duma, the war industries committees, and so forth.

The Guchkov government is held in a vice: bound by the interests of capital, it is compelled to strive to continue the predatory, robber war, to protect the monstrous profits of capital and the landlords, to restore the monarchy. Bound by its revolutionary origin and by the need for an abrupt change from tsarism to democracy, pressed by the bread-hungry and peace-hungry masses, the government is compelled to lie, to wriggle, to play for time, to 'proclaim' and promise (promises are the only things that are very cheap even at a time of madly rocketing prices) as much as possible and do as little as possible, to make concessions with one hand and to withdraw them with the other.

Under certain circumstances, the new government can at best postpone its collapse somewhat by leaning on all the organizing ability of the entire Russian bourgeoisie and bourgeois intelligentsia. But even in that case it is *unable* to avoid collapse, because it is *impossible* to escape from the claws of the terrible monster of imperialist war and famine nurtured by world capitalism unless one renounces bourgeois relationships, passes to revolutionary measures, appeals to the supreme historic heroism of both the Russian and world proletariat.

Hence the conclusion: we cannot overthrow the new government at one stroke, or, if we can (in revolutionary times the limits of what is possible expand a thousandfold), we will not be able to maintain power *unless we counter* the magnificent organization of the entire Russian bourgeoisie and the entire bourgeois intelligentsia with an equally magnificent *organization of the proletariat*, which must lead the entire vast mass of urban and rural poor, the semi-proletariat and small proprietors.

Irrespective of whether the 'second revolution' has already broken out in St Petersburg (I have said that it would be absolutely absurd to think that it is possible from abroad to assess the actual tempo at which it is maturing), whether it has been postponed for some time, or whether it has already begun in individual areas (of which some signs are evident)—in *any* case, the slogan of the moment on the eve of the new revolution, during it, and on the morrow of it, must be *proletarian organization*.

Comrade workers! You performed miracles of proletarian heroism yesterday in overthrowing the tsarist monarchy. In the more or less near future (perhaps even now, as these lines are being written) you will again have to perform the same miracles of heroism to overthrow the rule of the landlords and capitalists, who are waging the imperialist war. You will not achieve *durable victory* in this next 'real' revolution if you do not perform *miracles of proletarian organization!*

Organization is the slogan of the moment. But to confine oneself to that is to say nothing, for, on the one hand, organization is *always* needed; hence, mere reference to the necessity of 'organizing the masses' explains absolutely nothing. On the other hand, he who confines himself solely to this becomes an abettor of the liberals, for the *very thing* the *liberals* want in order to strengthen their rule is that the workers *should not go beyond their ordinary* 'legal' (from the standpoint of 'normal' bourgeois society) organizations, i.e., that they should *only* join their party, their trade union, their co-operative society, etc., etc.

Guided by their class instinct, the workers have realized that in revolutionary times they need *not only* ordinary, but an entirely different organization.

They have rightly taken the path indicated by the experience of our 1905 Revolution and of the 1871 Paris Commune; they have set up a *Soviet of Workers' Deputies*; they have begun to develop, expand and strengthen it by drawing in soldiers' deputies, and, undoubtedly, deputies from rural wage-workers, and then (in one form or another) from the entire peasant poor.

The prime and most important task, and one that brooks no delay, is to set up organizations of this kind in all parts of Russia without exception, for all trades and strata of the proletarian and semi-proletarian population without exception, i.e., for all the working and exploited people, to use a less economically exact but more popular term. Running ahead somewhat, I shall mention that for the entire mass of the peasantry our Party (its *special* role in the new type of proletarian organizations I hope to discuss in one of my next letters) should especially recommend Soviets of wage-workers and Soviets of small tillers who do not sell grain, to be formed *separately* from the well-to-do peasants. Without this, it will be impossible either to conduct a truly proletarian policy in general,[13] or correctly to approach the extremely important practical question which is a matter of life and death for millions of people: the proper distribution of *grain*, increasing its production, etc.

It might be asked: What should be the function of the Soviets of Workers' Deputies? They 'must be regarded as organs of insurrection, of revolutionary rule', we wrote in No. 47 of the Geneva *Sotsial-Demokrat*, of 13 October 1915.

This theoretical proposition, deduced from the experience of the Commune of 1871 and of the Russian Revolution of 1905, must be explained and concretely developed on the basis of the practical experience of precisely the present stage of the present revolution in Russia.

---

13 *Lenin's note*: In the rural districts a struggle will now develop for the small and, partly, middle peasants. The landlords, leaning on the well-to-do peasants, will try to lead them into subordination to the bourgeoisie. Leaning on the rural wage-workers and rural poor, we must lead them into the closest alliance with the urban proletariat.

We need revolutionary *government*, we need (for a certain transitional period) a *state*. This is what distinguishes us from the anarchists. The difference between the revolutionary Marxists and the anarchists is not only that the former stand for centralized, large-scale communist production, while the latter stand for disconnected small production. The difference between us precisely on the question of government, of the state, is that we are *for*, and the anarchists *against*, utilizing revolutionary forms of the state in a revolutionary way for the struggle for socialism.

We need a state. But *not the kind* of state the bourgeoisie has created everywhere, from constitutional monarchies to the most democratic republics. And in this we differ from the opportunists and Kautskyites of the old, and decaying, socialist parties, who have distorted, or have forgotten, the lessons of the Paris Commune and the analysis of these lessons made by Marx and Engels.[14]

---

14 *Lenin's note*: In one of my next letters, or in a special article, I will deal in detail with this analysis, given

We need a state, but not the kind the bourgeoisie needs, with organs of government in the shape of a police force, an army and a bureaucracy (officialdom) separate from and opposed to the people. All bourgeois revolutions merely perfected *this* state machine, merely transferred *it* from the hands of one party to those of another.

The proletariat, on the other hand, if it wants to uphold the gains of the present revolution and proceed further, to win peace, bread and freedom, must '*smash*', to use Marx's expression, this 'ready-made' state machine and substitute a new one for it by *merging* the police force, the army and the bureaucracy with the *entire armed people*. Following the path indicated by the experience of the Paris Commune of 1871 and the Russian Revolution of 1905, the proletariat must

---

in particular in Marx's *The Civil War in France*, in Engels's preface to the third edition of that work, in the letters: Marx's of 12 April 1871, and Engels's of 18-28 March 1875, and also with the utter distortion of Marxism by Kautsky in his controversy with Pannekoek in 1912 on the question of the so-called 'destruction of the state'.

organize and arm *all* the poor, exploited sections of the population in order that they *themselves* should take the organs of state power directly into their own hands, in order that *they themselves should constitute* these organs of state power.

And the workers of Russia have already taken this path in the first stage of the first revolution, in February–March 1917. The whole task now is clearly to understand what this new path is, to proceed along it further, boldly, firmly and perseveringly.

The Anglo-French and Russian capitalists wanted 'only' to remove, or only to 'frighten', Nicholas II, and to leave intact the old state machine, the police force, the army and the bureaucracy.

The workers went further and smashed it. And now, not only the Anglo-French, but also the German capitalists are *howling* with rage and horror as they see, for example, Russian soldiers shooting their officers, as in the case of Admiral Nepenin, that supporter of Guchkov and Milyukov.

I said that the workers have smashed the old state machine. It would be more correct to say: *have begun* to smash it.

In St Petersburg and in many other places the police force has been partly wiped out and partly dissolved. The Guchkov-Milyukov government *cannot* either restore the monarchy or, in general, maintain power *without restoring* the police force as a special organization of armed men under the command of the bourgeoisie, separate from and opposed to the people. That is as clear as daylight.

On the other hand, the new government must reckon with the revolutionary people, must feed them with half-concessions and promises, must play for time. That is why it resorts to half-measures: it establishes a 'people's militia' with elected officials (this sounds awfully respectable, awfully democratic, revolutionary and beautiful!) —*but ... but*, firstly, it places this militia under the control of the rural and urban local government bodies, i.e., under the command of landlords and capitalists who have been elected in conformity with laws passed by Nicholas the

Bloody and Stolypin the Hangman!! Secondly, although it calls it a 'people's militia' in order to throw dust in the eyes of the 'people', it does *not* call upon the *entire* people to join this militia, *and does not compel* the employers and capitalists to *pay* workers and office employees their ordinary wages *for the hours and days* they spend in the *public service*, i.e., in the militia.

That's their trick. That is how the landlord and capitalist government of the Guchkovs and Milyukovs manages to have a 'people's militia' on paper, while in reality it is restoring, gradually and on the quiet, the *bourgeois*, anti-people's militia. At first it is to consist of 'eight thousand students and professors' (as foreign newspapers describe the present St Petersburg militia)—an obvious plaything!—and will gradually be built up of the old and new *police force*.

Prevent restoration of the police force! Do not let the local government bodies slip out of your hands! Set up a militia that will really embrace the entire people, be really universal, and be led by the proletariat!—such is the task of the day, such is the slogan of the moment which equally conforms with the properly understood interests of furthering the class struggle, furthering the revolutionary movement, and the democratic instinct of every worker, of every peasant, of every exploited toiler who cannot help hating the policemen, the rural police patrols, the village constables, the command of landlords and capitalists over armed men with power over the people.

What kind of police force do *they* need, the Guchkovs and Milyukovs, the landlords and capitalists? The same kind as existed under the tsarist monarchy. After the briefest revolutionary periods, *all* the bourgeois and bourgeois-democratic republics in the world set up or restored *precisely such* a police force, a special organization of armed men subordinate to the bourgeoisie in one way or another, separate from and opposed to the people.

What kind of militia do we need, the proletariat, all the toiling people? A genuine *people's* militia, i.e., one that, first, consists of the *entire* population, of all adult citizens of *both* sexes;

and, second, one that combines the functions of a people's army with police functions, with the functions of the chief and fundamental organ of public order and public administration.

To make these propositions more comprehensible I will take a purely schematic example. Needless to say, it would be absurd to think of drawing up any kind of a 'plan' for a proletarian militia: when the workers and the entire people set about it practically, on a truly mass scale, they will work it out and organize it a hundred times better than any theoretician. I am not offering a 'plan', I only want to illustrate my idea.

St Petersburg has a population of about two million. Of these, more than half are between the ages of fifteen and sixty-five. Take half—one million. Let us even subtract an entire fourth as physically unfit, etc., taking no part in public service at the present moment for justifiable reasons. There remain 750,000 who, serving in the militia, say, one day in fifteen (and receiving their pay for this time from their employers), would form an army of 50,000.

That's the type of 'state' we need!

That's the kind of militia that would be a 'people's militia' in deed and not only in words.

That is how we must proceed in order to *prevent* the restoration either of a special police force, or of a special army separate from the people.

Such a militia, 95 hundredths of which would consist of workers and peasants, would express the *real* mind and will, the strength and power of the vast majority of the people. Such a militia would really arm, and provide military training for, the entire people, would be a safeguard, but *not* of the Guchkov or Milyukov type, against all attempts to restore reaction, against all the designs of tsarist agents. Such a militia would be the executive organ of the Soviets of Workers' and Soldiers' Deputies, it would enjoy the *boundless* respect and confidence of the people, for it itself would be an organization of the entire people. Such a militia would transform democracy from a beautiful signboard, which covers up the enslavement and torment of the people by the capitalists, into a means of actually *training the masses* for participation in *all* affairs of state. Such a militia would draw the young people into political life and teach them not only by words, but also by action, by *work*. Such a militia would develop those functions which, speaking in scientific language, come within the purview of the 'welfare police', sanitary inspection, and so forth, and would enlist for such work all adult women. If women are not drawn into public service, into the militia, into political life, if women are not torn out of their stupefying house and kitchen environment, it will be *impossible* to guarantee real freedom, it will be *impossible* to build even democracy, let alone socialism.

Such a militia would be a proletarian militia, for the industrial and urban workers would exert a guiding influence on the masses of the poor as naturally and inevitably as they came to hold the leading place in the people's revolutionary struggle both in 1905–07 and in 1917.

Such a militia would ensure absolute order and devotedly observed comradely discipline. At the same time, in the severe crisis that all the belligerent countries are experiencing, it would make it possible to combat this crisis in a very democratic way, properly and rapidly to distribute grain and other supplies, introduce 'universal labour service', which the French now call 'civilian mobilization' and the Germans 'civilian service', and without which *it is impossible—it has proved to be impossible*—to heal the wounds that have been and are being inflicted by the predatory and horrible war.

Has the proletariat of Russia shed its blood only in order to receive fine promises of political democratic reforms, and nothing more? Can it be that it will not demand, and secure, that *every* toiler should *forthwith* see and feel some improvement in his life? That every family should have bread? That every child should have a bottle of good milk, and that not a single adult in a rich family should dare take extra milk until children are provided for? That the palaces and rich apartments abandoned by the tsar and the aristocracy should not remain vacant, but provide shelter for the homeless and the destitute? Who can carry out these measures except a people's militia, to which women must belong equally with men?

These measures *do not yet* constitute socialism. They concern the distribution of consumption, not the reorganization of production. They would not yet constitute the 'dictatorship of the proletariat', only the 'revolutionary-democratic dictatorship of the proletariat and the poor peasantry'. It is not a matter of finding a theoretical classification. We would be committing a great mistake if we attempted to force the complete, urgent, rapidly developing practical tasks of the revolution into the Procrustean bed of narrowly conceived 'theory', instead of regarding theory primarily and predominantly as a *guide to action*.

Do the masses of the Russian workers possess sufficient class-consciousness, fortitude and heroism to perform 'miracles of proletarian organization' after they have performed miracles of daring, initiative and self-sacrifice in the direct revolutionary struggle? That we do not know, and it would be idle to indulge in guessing, for practice *alone* furnishes the answers to such questions.

What we do know definitely—and what we, as a party, must explain to the masses—is, on the one hand, the immense power of the locomotive of history that is engendering an unprecedented crisis, starvation and incalculable hardship. That locomotive is the war, waged for predatory aims by the capitalists of *both* belligerent camps. This 'locomotive' has brought a number of the richest, freest and most enlightened nations to the brink of doom. It is *forcing* the peoples to strain to the utmost all their energies, placing them in unbearable conditions, putting on the order of the day not the application of certain 'theories' (an illusion against which Marx always warned socialists), but implementation of the most extreme practical measures; for *without* extreme measures, death—immediate and certain death from starvation—awaits millions of people.

That the revolutionary enthusiasm of the advanced class can do a *great deal* when the objective situation *demands* extreme measures from the entire people, needs no proof. *This* aspect is clearly seen and *felt* by everybody in Russia.

It is important to realize that in revolutionary times the objective situation changes with the same swiftness and abruptness as the current of life in general. And we must *be able to adapt* our tactics and immediate tasks to the *specific features* of every given situation. Before February 1917, the immediate task was to conduct bold revolutionary internationalist propaganda, summon the masses to fight, rouse them. The February–March days required the heroism of devoted struggle to crush the immediate enemy—tsarism. Now we are in *transition* from that first stage of the revolution to the second, from 'coming to grips' with tsarism to 'coming to grips' with Guchkov–Milyukov land-lord and capitalist imperialism. The immediate task is *organization*, not only in the stereotyped sense of working to form stereotyped organiza-tions, but in the sense of drawing unprecedent-edly broad masses of the oppressed classes into an organization that would take over the military, political and economic functions of the state.

The proletariat has approached, and will approach, this singular task in different ways.

In some parts of Russia the February–March Revolution puts nearly complete power in its hands. In others the proletariat may, perhaps, in a 'usurpatory' manner, begin to form and develop a proletarian militia. In still others, it will probably strive for immediate elections of urban and rural local government bodies on the basis of universal, etc., suffrage, in order to turn them into revolutionary centres, etc., until the growth of proletarian organization, the coming together of the soldiers with the workers, the movement among the peasantry and the disillusionment of very many in the war-imperialist government of Guchkov and Milyukov, bring near the hour when this government will be replaced by the 'government' of the Soviet of Workers' Deputies.

Nor ought we to forget that close to St Petersburg we have one of the most advanced, factually republican countries, namely, Finland, which, from 1905 to 1917, shielded by the revolutionary battles of Russia, has in a relatively peaceful way developed democracy, and has won the *majority* of the people for socialism. The Russian proletariat will guarantee the Finnish Republic complete freedom, including freedom to secede (it is doubtful now whether a single Social-Democrat will waver on this point when the Cadet Rodichev is so meanly haggling in Helsingfors for bits of privileges for the Great Russians)—and, precisely in this way, will win the *complete* confidence and comradely assistance of the Finnish workers for the all-Russian proletarian cause. In a difficult and big undertaking, mistakes are inevitable, nor will we avoid them. The Finnish workers are better organizers, they will help us in this sphere, they will, *in their own way*, push forward the establishment of the socialist republic.

Revolutionary victories in Russia proper—peaceful organizational successes in Finland shielded by these victories—the Russian workers' transition to revolutionary organizational tasks on a new scale—capture of power by the proletariat and poorest strata of the population—encouragement and development of the socialist revolution in the West—this is the road that will lead us to *peace* and *socialism*.

N. Lenin

Zurich, 11 (24) March 1917

Fourth Letter

How to achieve peace

have just (March 12/25) read in the *Neue Zürcher Zeitung* (No. 517 of 24 March) the following telegraphic dispatch from Berlin:

It is reported from Sweden that Maxim Gorky has sent the government and the Executive Committee greetings couched in enthusiastic terms. He greets the people's victory over the lords of reaction and calls upon all Russia's sons to help erect the edifice of the new Russian state. At the same time he urges the government to crown the cause of emancipation by concluding peace.

It must not, he says, be peace at any price; Russia now has less reason than ever to strive for peace at any price. It must be a peace that will enable Russia to live in honour among the other nations of the earth. Mankind has shed much blood; the new government would render not only Russia, but all mankind, the greatest service if it succeeded in concluding an early peace.

That is how Maxim Gorky's letter is reported.

It is with deep chagrin that one reads this letter, impregnated through and through with stock philistine prejudices. The author of these lines has had many occasions, in meetings with Gorky in Capri, to warn and reproach him for his political mistakes. Gorky parried these reproaches with his inimitable charming smile and with the ingenuous remark: 'I know I am a bad Marxist. And besides, we artists are all somewhat irresponsible.' It is not easy to argue against that.

There can be no doubt that Gorky's is an enormous artistic talent which has been, and will be, of great benefit to the world proletarian movement.

But why should Gorky meddle in politics?

In my opinion, Gorky's letter expresses prejudices that are exceedingly widespread not only among the petty bourgeoisie, but also among a section of the workers under its influence. *All* the energies of our Party, all the efforts of the class-conscious workers, must be concentrated on a persistent, persevering, all-round struggle against these prejudices.

The tsarist government began and waged the present war as an *imperialist*, predatory war to rob and strangle weak nations. The government of the Guchkovs and Milyukovs, which is a landlord and capitalist government, is forced to continue, and wants to continue, *this very same kind* of war. To urge that government to conclude a democratic peace is like preaching virtue to brothel keepers.

Let me explain what is meant.

What is imperialism?

In my *Imperialism, the Highest Stage of Capitalism*, the manuscript of which was delivered to Parus Publishers some time before the revolution, was accepted by them and announced in the magazine *Letopis*,[15] I answered this question as follows:

> Imperialism is capitalism at that stage of development at which the dominance of monopolies and finance capital is established; in which the export of capital has acquired pronounced importance; in which the division of the world among the international trusts has begun; in which the division of all territories of the globe among the biggest capitalist powers has been completed. (Chapter VII of the above-mentioned book, the publication of which was announced in *Letopis*, when the censorship still existed, under the title *Modern Capitalism*, by V. Ilyin).

The whole thing hinges on the fact that capital has grown to huge dimensions. Associations of

---

15 *Imperialism, the Highest Stage of Capitalism* was written in the first half of 1916 and finally published in mid-1917, with a preface by Lenin dated 26 April. Parus (Sail) and *Letopis* (Annals) were the publishing house and magazine founded by Gorky in Petrograd.

a small number of the biggest capitalists (cartels, syndicates, trusts) manipulate billions, and divide the whole world among themselves.

The world has been *completely* divided up. The war was brought on by the clash of the two most powerful groups of multimillionaires, Anglo-French and German, for the *redivision* of the world.

The Anglo-French group of capitalists wants first to rob Germany, deprive her of her colonies (nearly all of which have already been seized), and then to rob Turkey.

The German group of capitalists wants to seize Turkey for itself and to compensate *itself* for the loss of its colonies by seizing neighbouring small states (Belgium, Serbia, Romania).

This is the real truth; it is being concealed by all sorts of bourgeois lies about a 'liberating', 'national' war, a 'war for right and justice', and similar jingles with which the capitalists always fool the common people.

Russia is waging this war with foreign money. Russian capital is a *partner* of Anglo-French capital. Russia is waging the war in order to rob Armenia, Turkey, Galicia.

Guchkov, Lvov and Milyukov, our present ministers, are not chance comers. They are the representatives and leaders of the entire landlord and capitalist class. They are *bound* by the interests of capital. The capitalists can no more renounce their interests than a man can lift himself by his bootstraps.

Secondly, Guchkov-Milyukov and Co. are *bound* by Anglo-French capital. They have waged, and are still waging, the war with foreign money. They have borrowed billions, promising to pay *hundreds of millions* in interest *every year*, and to squeeze this *tribute* out of the Russian workers and Russian peasants.

Thirdly, Guchkov-Milyukov and Co. are *bound* to England, France, Italy, Japan and other groups of robber capitalists by direct *treaties* concerning the predatory aims of this war. These treaties were concluded by *Tsar Nicholas II*. Guchkov-Milyukov and Co. took advantage of the workers' struggle against the tsarist monarchy to seize power, and *they have confirmed the treaties* concluded by the tsar.

This was done by the whole of the Guchkov-Milyukov government in a Manifesto which the St Petersburg Telegraph Agency circulated on 7 (20) March: 'The government [of Guchkov and Milyukov] will faithfully abide by all the treaties that bind us with other powers', says the Manifesto. Milyukov, the new Minister for Foreign Affairs, said the same thing in his telegram of 5 (18) March 1917 to all Russian representatives abroad.

These are all *secret* treaties, and Milyukov and Co. *refuse* to make them public for two reasons: (1) they fear the people, who are opposed to the predatory war; (2) they are bound by Anglo-French capital, which insists that the treaties remain secret. But every newspaper reader who has followed events knows that these treaties envisage the robbery of China by Japan; of Persia, Armenia, Turkey (especially Constantinople) and Galicia by Russia; of Albania by Italy; of Turkey and the German colonies by France and England, etc.

This is how things stand.

Hence, to urge the Guchkov-Milyukov government to conclude a speedy, honest, democratic and good-neighbourly peace is like the good village priest urging the landlords and the merchants to 'walk in the way of God', to love their neighbours and to turn the other cheek. The landlords and merchants listen to these sermons, continue to oppress and rob the people, and praise the priest for his ability to console and pacify the 'muzhiks'.

Exactly the same role is played—consciously or unconsciously—by all those who, in the present imperialist war, address pious peace appeals to the bourgeois governments. The bourgeois governments either refuse to listen to such appeals, and even prohibit them, or they allow them to be made, and assure all and sundry that they are fighting only to conclude the speediest and 'justest' peace, and that all the blame lies with the enemy. Actually, talking peace *to bourgeois* governments turns out to be *deception of the people*.

The groups of capitalists who have drenched

the world in blood for the sake of dividing territories, markets and concessions cannot conclude an 'honourable' peace. They can conclude only a shameful peace, a peace based on the division of the spoils, on the partition of Turkey and the colonies. Moreover, the Guchkov-Milyukov government is in general opposed to peace at the present moment, because the '*only*' 'loot' it would get now would be Armenia and part of Galicia, whereas it *also* wants to get Constantinople *and* regain from the Germans Poland, which tsarism has always so inhumanly and shamelessly oppressed.

Further, the Guchkov-Milyukov government is, in essence, only the agent of Anglo-French capital, which wants to retain the colonies it has wrested from Germany and, *on top of that*, compel Germany to hand back Belgium and part of France. Anglo-French capital helped the Guchkovs and Milyukovs to remove Nicholas II in order that they might help it to 'vanquish' Germany.

What, then, is to be done?

To achieve peace (and still more to achieve a really democratic, a really honourable peace), it is necessary that political power be in the hands of *the workers and poorest peasants*, not the landlords and capitalists. The latter represent an insignificant minority of the population, and the capitalists, as everybody knows, are making fantastic profits out of the war.

The workers and poorest peasants are the *vast* majority of the population. They are not making profit out of the war; on the contrary, they are being reduced to ruin and starvation. They are bound neither by capital nor by the treaties between the predatory groups of capitalists; they can and sincerely want to end the war.

If political power in Russia were in the hands of the *Soviets* of Workers', Soldiers' and Peasants' Deputies, these Soviets, and the *All-Russia Soviet* elected by them, could, and no doubt would, agree to carry out the peace programme which our Party (the Russian Social-Democratic Labour Party) outlined as early as 13 October 1915, in No. 47 of its Central Organ, *Sotsial-Demokrat* (then published in Geneva because of the draconic tsarist censorship).

This programme would probably be the following:

(1) The All-Russia Soviet of Workers', Soldiers' and Peasants' Deputies (or the St Petersburg Soviet temporarily acting for it) would forthwith declare that it is not bound by *any* treaties concluded *either* by the tsarist monarchy *or* by the bourgeois governments.

(2) It would forthwith publish *all* these treaties in order to hold up to public shame the predatory aims of the tsarist monarchy and of *all* the bourgeois governments without exception.

(3) It would forthwith publicly call upon *all* the belligerent powers to conclude an *immediate armistice*.

(4) It would immediately bring to the knowledge of all the people our, the workers' and peasants' peace *terms*: liberation of *all* colonies; liberation of *all* dependent, oppressed and unequal nations.

(5) It would declare that it expects nothing

good from the bourgeois governments, and calls upon the workers of all countries to overthrow them and to transfer all political power to Soviets of Workers' Deputies.

(6) It would declare that the *capitalist gentry themselves* can repay the billions of debts contracted by the bourgeois governments to wage this criminal, predatory war, and that the workers and peasants *refuse to recognize* these debts. To pay the interest on these loans would mean paying the capitalists *tribute* for many years for having graciously allowed the workers to kill one another in order that the capitalists might divide the spoils.

Workers and peasants!—the Soviet of Workers' Deputies would say—Are you willing to pay these gentry, the capitalists, *hundreds of millions* of roubles *every year* for a war waged for the division of the African colonies, Turkey, etc.?

For *these* peace terms the Soviet of Workers' Deputies would, in my opinion, agree to *wage war* against *any* bourgeois government and against *all* the bourgeois governments of the world, because this would really be a just war, because *all* the workers and toilers in *all* countries would *work for its success.*

The German worker now sees that the bellicose monarchy in Russia is being replaced by a bellicose republic, a republic of capitalists who want to continue the imperialist war, and who have confirmed the predatory treaties of the tsarist monarchy.

Judge for yourselves: can the German worker trust *such* a republic?

Judge for yourselves: can the war continue, can the capitalist domination continue on earth, if the Russian people, always sustained by the living memories of the great Revolution of 1905, win complete freedom and transfer all political power to the Soviets of Workers' and Peasants' Deputies?

N. Lenin

Zurich, 12 (25) March 1917

Fifth Letter

The tasks involved in the building of the revolutionary proletarian state

In the preceding letters, the immediate tasks of the revolutionary proletariat in Russia were formulated as follows: (1) to find the surest road to the next stage of the revolution, or to the second revolution, which (2) must transfer political power from the government of the landlords and capitalists (the Guchkovs, Lvovs, Milyukovs, Kerenskys) to a government of the workers and poorest peasants. (3) This latter government must be organized on the model of the Soviets of Workers' and Peasants' Deputies, namely, (4) it must smash, completely eliminate, the old state machine, the army, the police force and bureaucracy (officialdom) that is common to *all* bourgeois states, and substitute for this machine (5) not only a mass organization, but a universal organization of the entire armed people. (6) *Only* such a government, of 'such' a class composition ('revolutionary-democratic dictatorship of the proletariat and peasantry'), and such organs of government ('proletarian militia') *will be capable* of successfully carrying out the extremely difficult and absolutely urgent *chief* task of the moment, namely: to achieve *peace*—not an imperialist peace, not a deal between the imperialist powers concerning the division of the booty by the capitalists and their governments, but a really lasting and democratic peace, which cannot be achieved without a proletarian revolution in a number of countries. (7) In Russia, the victory of the proletariat can be achieved in the very near future *only* if, from the very first step, the workers are supported by the vast majority of the peasants fighting for the confiscation of the landed estates (and for the nationalization of all the land, if we assume that the agrarian programme of the '104' is still essentially the agrarian programme of the *peasantry*[16]). (8) In connection with such a

---

16 The agrarian programme of the '104' was a land reform bill submitted by the Trudovik members to the thirteenth meeting of the First State Duma on 23 May (5

peasant revolution, and on its basis, the proletariat can and must, in alliance with the *poorest* section of the peasantry, take further steps towards *control* of the production and distribution of the basic products, towards the introduction of 'universal labour service', etc. These steps are dictated, with absolute inevitability, by the conditions created by the war, which in many respects will become still more acute in the post-war period. In their entirety and in their development these steps will mark the *transition to socialism*, which cannot be achieved in Russia directly, at one stroke, without transitional measures, but is quite achievable and urgently necessary as a result of such transitional measures. (9) In this connection, the task of immediately organizing special Soviets of Workers' Deputies in the *rural districts*, i.e., Soviets of agricultural wage-workers *separate* from the Soviets of the other peasant deputies, comes to the forefront with extreme urgency.

June) 1906. The land would belong to the entire people, and farmlands would be allowed only to those tilling them by their own labour.

Such, briefly, is the programme we have outlined, based on an appraisal of the class forces in
the Russian and world revolution, and also on
the experience of 1871 and 1905.

Let us now attempt a general survey of this
programme as a whole and, in passing, deal
with the way the subject was approached by K.
Kautsky, the chief theoretician of the 'Second'
(1889–1914) International and most prominent
representative of the 'Centre', 'marsh' trend that
is now to be observed in all countries, the trend
that oscillates between the social-chauvinists and
the revolutionary internationalists. Kautsky discussed this subject in his magazine *Die Neue Zeit*
of 6 April 1917 (new style) in an article entitled
'The Prospects of the Russian Revolution'.

'First of all', writes Kautsky, 'we must ascertain
what tasks confront the revolutionary proletarian
regime' (state system).

'Two things', continues the author, 'are
urgently needed by the proletariat: democracy
and socialism.'

Unfortunately, Kautsky advances this absolutely

incontestable thesis in an exceedingly general form, so that in essence he says nothing and explains nothing. Milyukov and Kerensky, members of a bourgeois and imperialist government, would readily subscribe to this general thesis—one to the first part, and the other to the second ...[17]

---

17 The manuscript breaks off here.—*Ed.*